D1269325

THE SERPENT AND THE TORTOISE

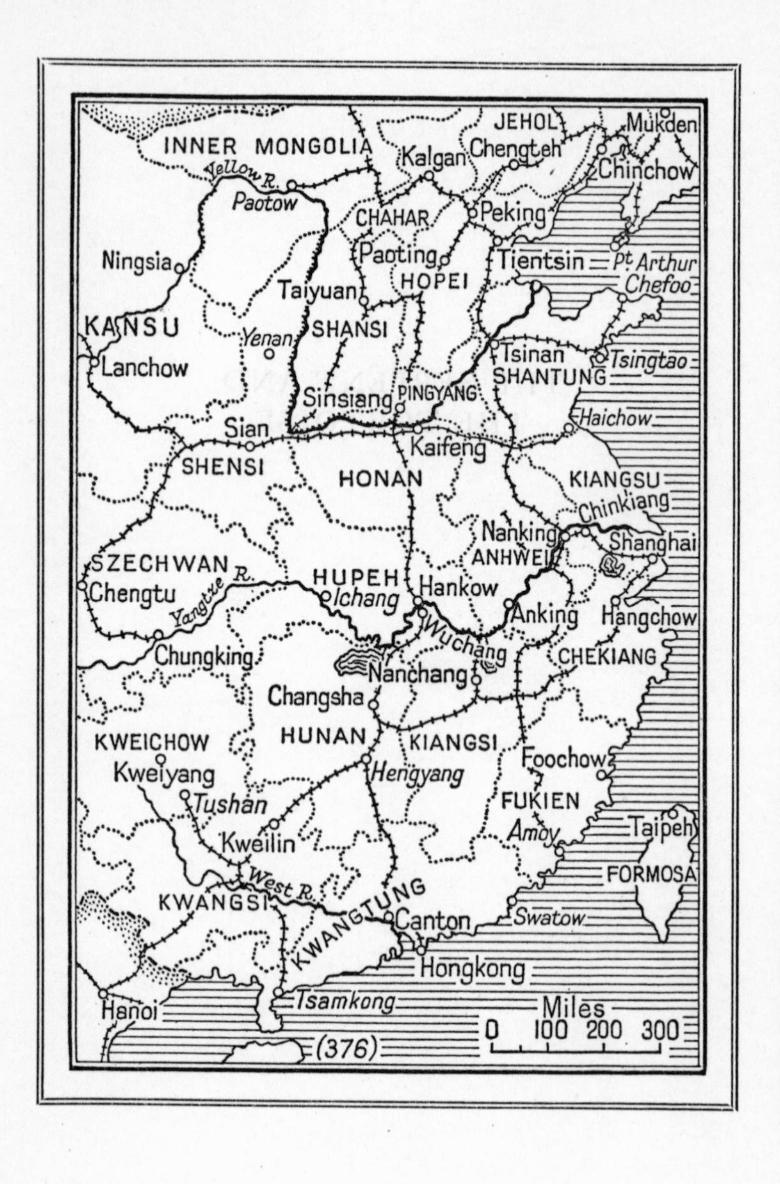

INNER MONGOLIA
JEHOL
Mukden
Kalgan
Chengteh
Chinchow
Yellow R.
Paotow
CHAHAR
Peking
Ningsia
Paoting
Tientsin
Pt. Arthur
HOPEI
Taiyuan
Chefoo
KANSU
Yenan
SHANSI
Lanchow
Tsinan
Tsingtao
SHANTUNG
Sinsiang
PINGYANG
Haichow
Sian
Kaifeng
SHENSI
HONAN
KIANGSU
Chinkiang
Nanking
Shanghai
ANHWEI
SZECHWAN
HUPEH
Chengtu
Yangtze R.
Ichang
Hankow
Anking
Hangchow
Wuchang
Chungking
CHEKIANG
Nanchang
Changsha
HUNAN
KIANGSI
KWEICHOW
Kweiyang
Hengyang
Foochow
Tushan
FUKIEN
Kweilin
Amoy
Taipeh
FORMOSA
West R.
KWANGSI
KWANGTUNG
Canton
Swatow
Hongkong
Hanoi
Tsamkong
Miles
0 100 200 300
(376)

THE SERPENT AND THE TORTOISE

Problems of the New China

BY

EDGAR FAURE
FORMER PRIME MINISTER OF FRANCE

TRANSLATED BY

LOVETT F. EDWARDS

NEW YORK
ST MARTIN'S PRESS
1958

MACMILLAN AND COMPANY LIMITED
London Bombay Calcutta Madras Melbourne

THE MACMILLAN COMPANY OF CANADA LIMITED
Toronto

ST MARTIN'S PRESS INC
New York

PRINTED IN GREAT BRITAIN

TRANSLATOR'S FOREWORD

M. Edgar Faure is the first Western statesman of standing to have visited both the Chinese People's Democratic Republic and the Soviet Union and to have written an account of his impressions and conclusions. He is singularly well qualified to do so. Twice Prime Minister of France, M. Faure has at various times been Minister of Foreign Affairs, of Justice and of Finance and Economic Affairs. A lawyer by training, M. Faure was in charge of the Legal Department of the Committee of Liberation in the Provisional Government of General de Gaulle in Algiers and later represented France at the Nuremburg trials. He has represented the Jura region in the National Assembly since 1946. He speaks Russian. He has travelled extensively and has visited the Soviet Union, including the Soviet Asiatic Republics. Last year he visited China at the invitation of the Chinese Government.

M. Faure looks at the problems of present-day China with the clarity and logic of an experienced statesman. He advocates a change in the present western attitude towards China and gives considered and logical reasons for such a change. He has discussed the external and internal problems of China with President Mao Tse-Tung and Foreign Minister and Premier Chou En-Lai; the problems of Formosa, of diplomatic recognition, of entry into the United Nations as one of the 'Big Five', and the internal political campaigns — the 'rectification' campaign, the 'Hundred Flowers', the counter-campaign against deviationists and the formation of the so-called 'mixed economy' — which have so often puzzled western observers.

It is uncommon for a western statesman to have had personal knowledge of both the Chinese and the Soviet leaders. M. Faure has this knowledge, and gives a striking comparison of the personalities of the two leaders of the communist world — Mao Tse-Tung and Nikita Khrushchev.

M. Faure's book was intended for French readers. But the problems he sets out and the conclusions that he reaches are equally applicable to the English and Americans. Before reaching a conclusion it is necessary to understand the facts and to be able to interpret them. M. Faure's book enables us to do so.

LOVETT F. EDWARDS

CONTENTS

PART THREE

PREFACE

IN OCTOBER 1955 I and my wife were invited to visit China by the Institute of Foreign Affairs. I replied that I could only consider doing so in the following spring. So when in February the invitation was kindly repeated, I decided to take advantage of it, and on Easter Monday set foot for the first time on the juridical territory of the Chinese People's Republic at its Embassy in Berne.

Encouraged by the counsels of Mr. Feng, and by a first (and favourable) experience of Chinese cooking and white rice-wine slightly reminiscent of Chateau-Chalon, and provided with loose-leaf visas, not intended as some believe to spare western passports a compromising and indelible stamp, we set out on May 13th by the longest way round — the excellent southern service of Air France.

My first stop was at Karachi, almost exactly half-way. I was thus enabled to make the acquaintance of President Iskander Mirza and to discuss China at great length with his energetic Prime Minister, Hussein Shahad Suhrawardy. Mr. Suhrawardy has made a trip to Pekin and has spent sixteen hours in conversation with Mao Tse-Tung and Chou En-Lai; he has also received Chou En-Lai in Pakistan. His opinion, like that of all serious observers, is that only the present régime was capable of bringing about the achievements that have taken place in China. This fair-minded judgment has in no way affected the firmness of his own non-communist views.

Mr. Suhrawardy is a contemporary of Mao Tse-Tung, though he appears younger than Chou En-Lai. He too is one of those statesmen who have attained world prominence during the past ten years, in the development of a remarkable career. As Mao Tse-Tung at one time governed in Yenan, so Mr. Suhrawardy at one time governed in Bengal, but to-day, paradoxically, he finds himself cut off, at the height of his career, from his native land.

Pakistan itself first came to its majority as a nation a little before modern China (1947). Less vast and less populous, it none the less prides itself because of its ninety million inhabitants on being the fifth country in the world, and we must not forget, as we do only too often, that it is by a long way the number one Moslem state. It has similar problems to confront; a most archaic economy and an overwhelming proportion of illiterates. It has undertaken to solve them by liberal and democratic methods. Its political life is becoming more intense, not without some confusion, at the approach of its first general elections, which are foreseen for the coming year. It has not yet settled the great questions of its future. Women there are sufficiently emancipated to have the vote; they will even vote once more than the men in order to assure in Parliament the guaranteed feminine representation (10 per cent); yet polygamy remains legal and the leaders themselves practice it.

Our second stop was naturally Hong Kong. Although the island of Hong Kong, with Kowloon and the New Territories, is famous for its site and its scenic beauties, it is still politically an extraordinary entity created by a variety of historical and juridical causes; cessions, treaty, long leases, with a régime that Sir Alexander Graham likes to define as a benevolent dictatorship by governor.

Because of Hong Kong, England has recognized China who has only half-recognized England but, because of England, China does not entirely claim Hong Kong. In this forward outpost of Empire, capitalism deploys the extreme seductions of complete laissez-faire and customs franchises, but China has installed there her warehouses, bank and safe-deposits and does her best business there (a hundred million pounds profit annually). The state-controlled merchant junks, in files of rust-coloured sails, come every morning to nourish this ant-hill of free enterprise. The Bank of China dominates from its tall tower the neighbouring English banks, the Law Courts and the square where the powerful Hong Kong-Shanghai Corporation has seen fit to re-erect the statue of its chairman, Thomas Jackson; but nearby the Chartered in its turn indulges in skyscraper competition, and French engineers are building a new and spacious aerodrome. Everywhere the fever of construction and investment is developing in a perfect uncertainty of what the morrow will bring.

Between Hong Kong and Canton one changes universes without changing continent or even province, but, on the other hand, frequently changing modes of locomotion. After the Kowloon ferry-boat, we followed the tourist road by car, with military tracks spreading on either side. We passed lorry-loads of soldiers, and guard-posts manned by Pakistani policemen and then, preceded by coolies carrying our luggage and crowned with huge hats over their red caps, we made our way on foot, as one must, across the railway bridge which is accessible only to foot passengers between the British station of Lowu and the Chinese station of Shumchun.

At the frontier, which is more like a line of demarcation and which astonishingly recalls memories of the forties to French travellers, Mr. Li, sent by the Institute of Foreign Affairs, and his interpreter, Mr. Tsia, were awaiting us (neither one nor the other, however, speaking the language of the province in which we were). We had now only to take our places in the meandering local railway which crawls along towards Canton when the permanent way is not blocked, at about fifteen miles an hour, crowded with Chinese men and women from overseas on family outings laden with foodstuffs of every conceivable sort.

Five weeks later, we left Pekin, this time by the shortest route, which M. Gascar calls 'the way of the heart', following the Russian civil airline to Prague on a TU 104, amidst Czech delegates carrying armfuls of flowers. We discovered Baikal at our first landing. At Irkutsk, an aerodrome official chatted with me about Béranger and Villon, about a treatise on aesthetics by Lefebvre and about the latest historical novel of my friend Maurice Druon; after leaving China, Siberia is already Europe. At Moscow, Mr. Gorchenin came to welcome us in the name of the Parliamentary delegation and at the aerodrome we had one of the seven or eight meals of the day, the first having been breakfast at Pekin and the last dinner with the family in Paris, where we arrived in broad daylight thanks to the prodigies of jet transport and the eccentricities of the time zones.

Being a politician, it is natural that my attention is mainly drawn to political problems, including questions of political economy. That is what my readers expect of me. I recall my reception at the Kremlin, in September 1956, by Nikita Khrushchev and Marshal Bulganin, and my hosts saying to me after the second or third toast: 'We are men of politics: then let us talk politics.' I think that it is this angle that my readers will expect to find in this account. In the course of my trip, I could not, naturally, remain insensible to the picturesque aspect of things, to the revelation of an unknown people and to a life so strange to us. Impressions of this type will appear, here and there, in the pages which follow. But, clearly, they will not be the main interest. A stay of five weeks is too short to sum up observations of a general nature and to strive to create something original. This has already been done by many books, useful and sometimes exhaustive, devoted to the new China. On the other hand it would be a great and entirely superfluous labour to write a theoretical study on the institutions and events of the new China with the aid of press cuttings, statistics and general information, which are so easily obtainable at Hong Kong, like a dish already prepared and which only needs to be heated up, seasoned and served. I have neither of these projects in view. A method of travelling like mine, even though not very official, is often made game of (I can none the less bear witness that my travels in China never had the least appearance of being Potemkin voyages), and would, indeed, be a handicap were it a question of a reportage. But, on the other hand, it is from my point of view an advantage, for political life necessarily and primarily involves — above all in the non-democratic countries — official life. I therefore propose, in the first section of these notes, to introduce the reader to the official circles of Pekin, to let him participate in my meetings with the Prime Minister, Chou En-Lai, and the President, Mao Tse-Tung, and other leading or not so leading personalities; and especially, if I may be permitted this licence, with Mr. L. W. M., an imaginary Chinese person, but one who holds only authentic views noted down almost literally.

In the second and third parts I will touch on the double question which has inspired my enquiries and which seems to me to justify this book. Is there such a thing as Chinese communism? If so, in what does it differ, politically or economically, from Soviet communism? Can one discern the design, or even the promise, of a third way, between dictatorship and democracy, between economic liberalism and absolute socialism? My reply, here and now, is in the negative. Communism in China is sharply distinguished from communism in the Soviet Union, but it is by methods, stages and institutions, not by aims or doctrines. Perhaps there will be, one day, a third way; this eventuality cannot be excluded, but its divergence will only become apparent when the asymptote will have fully rejoined the line of axis which it is approaching with a regular cadence and as if under the determination of a mathematical force. Chinese communism, if one may make use of this convenient term with the reserve that I have just set forth, is distinguished by its own individual institutions: in politics, the United Front: in economics, by the so-called mixed economy and the system of 'repurchase'. These institutions spring from a common root, which is the desire for the conquest and assimilation by the communist régime of those sections of the population which could be expected to be strangers to it and, therefore, prejudiced and hostile; that is to say the conquest and assimilation of the bourgeoisie, the business classes and intellectuals (a special chapter will be devoted to the parallel question of the religious cults). It is a policy of utilization, of adaptation, of recovery, inspired by the hope of retaining in the service of the régime everyone who could serve it effectively; the experts who are 'of value to our cause' and, if you will allow me to borrow a play on words from the terminology of Burnham, 'to manage the managers', the managers of intelligence and of industrial, financial or commercial technique. Therein lies the originality of method, therein lies the distinguishing mark of the system. If one can speak, as is sometimes done, of 'Mao Tse-Tungism' it is there that it finds its true definition. But I must repeat, it is a matter of 'communising the bourgeois' and in no way of 'bourgeoisising communism'. Such an undertaking cannot be conceived without difficulties, without shocks and without crises. These crises culminated, in the course of the last eight years, in the 'ideological remoulding' and the campaign known as the 'five antis'. We are now in course of experiencing a new one, which is still going on, the 'rectification campaign' and the counter-campaign against the right-wing deviationists, under the indeterminate standard of the 'Hundred Flowers'. We do not yet know the results of this campaign, which we shall study in the part devoted to politics, but we must not forget that these results are always only provisional. The results and the crisis itself are less important than the principle of development in cycles. Mao is an old horseman and there is a touch of 'dressage' in this affair. The régime uses a light rein or a curb according to whether it feels that it has reached a more or less advanced stage of success, whether it has or has not sufficiently reduced the risks of an unexpected reaction and according to the degree of confidence that it feels itself able, at any given moment, to place in others or test out for itself.

Finally, in these three parts — Visits and Interviews, Institutions and Political Campaigns, Economic Structure — in studying the basic problems of communist China, I will never forget for long the parallel problem of our own attitude towards communist China and the relations between capitalism and communism. Though I think that it is sure that China will not diverge from the path of political dictatorship and collectivist economy and that there is no indication of any third way, I remain firmly in favour of a fresh policy, more open, more assured and bolder, on the part of the western powers (and France in particular) towards the communist countries (and China in particular).

Such a policy seems to me to-day to be the policy of the best chance. Let us hope that the near future will not prove to us, too late, that it was the policy of the only chance.

This conclusion, which is touched on several times in different chapters, will be treated, as it should be, in the last one: The Future of Communism in China and East-West Relations. It is there too that the allegorical theme of the Serpent and the Tortoise will be explained. But, here and now, by placing at the beginning of this book extracts from two poems by Mao Tse-Tung (still unpublished in French), I have wished to present to the reader my two personages, in their immutable reality and in their symbolism.

In the land of China,
The nine-bedded river, the Yang Tse Kiang.

This shifting barrier
Divides the land, the North from the South. . . .
The Serpent and the Tortoise
Watch one another ages without end. . . .
While I, a wandering poet, let my gaze
Fall earthwards from the height of the tower.

(1937)

But the Serpent and the Tortoise
Keep their endless watch
And visions of times to come
Rise before my eyes. . . .
From the South bank to the North
Men will throw a bridge of iron.
They will forget that once was here
An impassable chasm.

(1956)

MAO TSE-TUNG

PART ONE

CHAPTER I

MR. CHANG HSI-JO — FIRST MEETINGS IN PEKIN

IN PEKIN I was the guest of the People's Institute for Foreign Affairs. It is what is known in China as a private organization. We would prefer to call it a semi-state organization. Its aim is to maintain relations between China and those countries with whom in fact she has no relations. It is an official agency of the Foreign Office with parallel diplomatic powers. In this matter the Chinese have not been able to seek inspiration from a Russian model, for it is now some time since the Soviet Union has almost completely restored the former network of diplomatic relations. It could, none the less, be a really typical Soviet idea! Furthermore, we can see that the Soviet Union makes great use of such organizations *sui generis*, such as the Parliamentary group, for parallel diplomatic and propaganda action.

By its very nature, the Institute for Foreign Affairs is not subject to the Minister who bears that title, nor to the many Assistant Ministers who exist in his department. Its President belongs, none the less, to the Chinese Government; he is Mr. Chang Hsi-Jo, Minister of Education. Do not think, however, that for this reason the Institute is concerned with cultural questions; for these there is another organization, the 'Bureau for Cultural Relations with Foreign Countries' which covers all countries 'recognized' or not, and which has the same Mr. Chang Hsi-Jo as Vice-President. Mr. Chang Hsi-Jo has been President of the Institute since it was founded in 1949, and only became Minister of Education later, in 1952. The combination of these powers is, therefore, personal and not functional.

The choice of Mr. Chang Hsi-Jo to conduct political relations with persons from the non-communist states is clearly a very happy one. His very appearance, his dress and his manners show him to be a statesman in the western sense. I have seen him more often dressed in the European manner with a sober elegance, but I have also met him wearing the long black Chinese tunic with distinction. He expresses himself fluently in English and very competently in French. He is one of those men who can serve as a bridge between two régimes — without, however, justifying the remark of Flaubert that certain men are like bridges; one passes over them without stopping. He is far from being a puppet personality chosen for reasons of window-dressing from the gallery of complaisant fellow-travellers of the old régime. His double career has predestined him for his double task; he won his revolutionary degrees by fighting at the age of nineteen in the Tung Meng Hui secret society founded by Sun Yat-Sen which plotted against the Manchu dynasty; he has since taken his place in university life, in administrative positions and in chairs of political science. He chose as his subject of study the Six Books of the Republic by Bodin.

The Minister of Education is a non-party man, cultivated and discreet, with a fine wit.

His statement during the 'rectification' campaign[1] was a little masterpiece of humour and wariness. At the time of the three 'isms', it was his task to formulate the distinction between 'laborious bureaucracy' smothered by excess of zeal and red tape and 'nonchalant bureaucracy' which led to the same negative results. A philosopher, he did not even in the first flush of the campaign harbour any illusion of a total victory: 'The flames cannot burn all the weeds; they will come up again with the spring winds.'

Mr. and Mrs. Chang Hsi-Jo were kind enough to ask us to their home, which is less unusual in Pekin than in Moscow. They lived on the ground floor of a pleasant house, once a

[1] For this campaign see Chapter X.

private residence, but now divided into flats. The way there led through a court and a garden. The windows of the library-study opened directly on to the river, the farther bank following the outer wall of the once Forbidden City, in fact a mediaeval moat. Everything was discreet luxury and order. The master of the house had lovingly placed on a number of small side-tables some delicate works of art, each one representative of a Chinese dynasty. Among them were three ancient statuettes, a lady, a dancer and a servant. Two were copies and one original. We were asked to guess which. (My wife is justly proud of recognizing at once the genuineness of the servant.) Mr. Chang Hsi-Jo's library was not for show but for work. He described to me, though as far as I was concerned it was an act of faith, the principles of a system which permitted him to find without difficulty those texts that he needed. Did the name of Ssu-Ma Chien turn up in conversation? Here was the reference, buried in one of those puzzle boxes that I could only with difficulty regard as books.

After his statuettes and his authors, Mr. Chang Hsi-Jo was glad to show us an album of photographs taken by him while in France and during a tour of Europe. What pleasanter recreation during those days of tension in Pekin than to breathe again, at the home of this eminent revolutionary, those flavours of classical culture and bourgeois holiday making?

I was almost at the end of my stay. What good was it to look back on familiar themes? Mr. Chang Hsi-Jo spoke of the past, but of a more recent past. He had, naturally, known Chiang Kai-Shek well. Like all the men of the new China who had come to maturity after the First World War, he had worked, hoped and waited under the Kuo Min Tang régime. He was one of those who had opened the fire of polemics at the same time as the fire of arms. He drew a parallel in the manner of Plutarch between Chiang Kai-Shek and the celebrated and ill-omened Yuan Shih-Kai, with whom Dr. Sun Yat-Sen, true to the Chinese genius for bargaining, had at one time made an inevitable and luckless bargain. But the imitation, he said, was ten times worse than the original. Was one to treat to-day with the Formosan Marshal? The genius for bargaining has not deserted China and there is something of Sun Yat-Sen in Chou En-Lai and more still, without doubt, in Mao Tse-Tung. But this time the trump cards are no longer with the new Yuan Shih-Kai.

Thinking of these negotiations, openly desired but not yet put in hand, there is one question that torments our western spirits accustomed to the intransigeance of public opinion. Should they eventually take place, should Chiang Kai-Shek agree to re-enter the régime, how will the public take this apostasy or, if one prefers, this hypostasy? How could this anger fanned to fever heat by curses and campaigns be suddenly appeased? One can only think that the communist régime possesses the secrets of Aeolus.

Mr. Chang Hsi-Jo, from his knowledge of the psychology of Chiang, did not believe in the success of the soundings now in course. But in the Chinese conception, it is the man who has faith and fervour who comes to terms in the supreme interest of his cause, rather than the careerist and the cynic. If one, none the less, succeeds surely that is all to the good? How many spiny questions are solved at a single blow! Then, assuredly, the public too will accept, and will agree to seeing Chiang Kai-Shek return to the stage in all the majesty of a governor, will see the traitor become 'a good fellow', like an actor changing his make-up in the Pekin Opera. Perhaps he will even get a round of applause; in any case, his is the leading part.

It was naturally the task of the Institute for Foreign Affairs to organize our first reception in the capital the day after our arrival. Dinner had been fixed for eight o'clock out of regard for western custom (the Chinese dine earlier). To get there we did not have to leave the Pekin Hotel where we were staying, but only to wander zigzag by corridors and lifts, for the hotel is composed of two blocks of buildings, the former French establishment and a built-on wing of colossal and Soviet conception. There were forty or fifty guests, the men in dark suits or Chinese tunics, a mark of equality, the women in evening dress, both in the European and Chinese style, and many very elegant. It was hard to find one's bearings in the orgy of introductions, the jumble of difficult names and complicated functions; individual conversations cut short and made even harder to follow by the necessity of an interpreter only allowed us with difficulty to know who was who, even after several meetings. Among the guests were all those who seemed to be Vice-Presidents of the Institute or connected with its activities, and also many men and women in politics, belonging to the small non-communist parties (several had already figured in the group which had welcomed us at the aerodrome). It is a trait of Chinese delicacy and also, no doubt, of well thought out propaganda to put the guests of the Institute, all non-communists, in touch with the representatives of those parties whose title of 'democratic' recalls to us, though from afar, our own loyalties.

The same principle is applied in the choice of delegates of the Institute in the provinces. I can still remember because of his age, his title and his rank, a Vice-President of the National Assembly who the day before had expressed to me the welcome of the parliamentarians, of whom I suppose him to be the doyen since he is a contemporary of my father; he had the long, sparse Chinese beard and belonged to the Party for Democratic Construction.[1] His expression was perpetually gay and sly, he had lived under four régimes and he had based his comparisons, of which one easily guessed the moral, on personal and direct experience.

Mr. Chang Hsi-Jo had placed me on his right for acoustic reasons; on my other side was the Assistant Minister of Foreign Affairs, a member of the Party. Facing me was Mr. Chang Po-Chun, Minister of Communications, recognizable by his heavy build. I could not then guess the notoriety that this hanger-on of a small party and manager of a technical

[1] The party of the won-over capitalists. Cf. Chapter VIII.

department was soon to find in the *cheng-feng* crisis[1] and in the campaign against right-wing deviationists.

If I 'marked down' that same evening among the guests another future deviationist, Mr. Lo Lung-Chi, of whom I shall have occasion to speak later, this was simply because his post as Minister of Forests would naturally attract the attention of a deputy of the Jura. Was the third rebel then in power, Mr. Chang Nai-Chi, Minister of Food Control, present? I cannot be sure. But, on the other hand, the two women ministers were both there; Madam Li Teh-Chuan, Minister of Public Health, who spoke both English and Russian (though without being able to pronounce the 'r') and who, on the occasion of the 'Hundred Flowers' campaign, undertook the defence of traditional Chinese medicine, and Madam Shih Liang, Minister of Justice, very beautiful and very chic, who spoke only Chinese but was accompanied by a polyglot husband. Neither has, since, been suspected of deviationism.

Formal banquets, according to the Chinese manner, have three things in their favour. Firstly, the skilled elaboration of the Chinese dishes saves them from the risk of mediocrity which is ever present in the west in the idea of banquet cuisine. Chinese cooking has always seemed to me extremely good even in little station buffets. As the number of guests grows larger, so the number of dishes increases also, without the size growing proportionately. Also, the service is always very fast, thanks to the simplicity in changing the couverts; twenty minutes for three or four persons and an hour and a quarter at the worst for the most official repast. Last but not least, speeches are made at the beginning of the banquet and not at the end.

In his introductory speech Mr. Chang Hsi-Jo devoted himself to retracing with the greatest accuracy all the initiatives I had been able to take and all the opinions I had been able to

[1] The so-called 'rectification' movement of a semi-liberal spirit turned on itself and reversed and, in the course of this change, several ministers found themselves accused. Cf. Chapter X.

express on China and Franco-Chinese relations. I mention here, and it will not be for the last time, how much the Chinese, who are believed to be little interested in affairs abroad, are most attentive and sensitive to all that concerns them. There is also a sentimental side to this, for the gesture that they found most to their taste and of which I was reminded later on several occasions, was when I had agreed to receive a Chinese youth delegation for a few moments at the Hotel Matignon. In my reply to Mr. Chang Hsi-Jo I felt bound to touch on a question that no one, clearly, would put to me but which a number of those present probably had in mind (it is true that I was reasoning along French lines). Since I had stressed on several occasions the lack of reality in western policy towards China and the paradox of the present diplomatic position, why had I not, as Prime Minister, taken the initiative of recognizing the Pekin government? It was simple for me to recall that the question of recognition was bound up with international questions; the problem of Formosa, the situation in the United Nations, etc. An isolated initiative could, consequently, be of less value than an advance towards a general settlement, which France considered desirable and for which she intended to use her influence.

In 1955 France had again been able to take the initiative on the international stage; she had instigated the meeting of the Four-Power Conference at Geneva and it would have been possible to foreshadow the discussion and settlement of the Chinese problem on that occasion had it lasted longer. But at the moment, it was necessary to abstain from any premature and incomplete action, which China would doubtless have greeted with the words: 'and if it pleases us not to be recognized?'

I saw from the expressions of those listening that they were grateful to me for these remarks and for approaching this problem openly; also, perhaps, for having understood certain paradoxes of their own policy.

But I thought to myself: 'Time has passed since 1955. Conditions are no longer what they were in the summer of that year. Since then we have been faced with the intransigeance of Mr. Molotov, principal (if not only) cause of the relative failure of the second Geneva meeting; then the collapse of French policy and the consequent wiping out of our diplomacy. Also many other events. In a general way, time has not worked for the great cause of common sense and happiness in the world. One must begin again from the beginning—at fresh expense. The reasoning and the solutions of yesterday are not necessarily valid to-day.' One must know what exactly it is that the Chinese want; that was to be made clear, less than twenty-four hours later, in my meeting with Chou En-Lai. One must also know what 'we westerns' and 'we French' can and must do. This will be, from time to time, the subject of my personal reflections in this book.

CHAPTER II

THE CHINESE KNOW HOW TO WAIT

Interview with Mr. Chou En-Lai

THE Prime Minister, Chou En-Lai, had, in fact, invited us to lunch the following day. We were to have the opportunity, during our stay, of meeting him several times.

The Prime Minister's residence, like that of the President, Mao Tse-Tung, and the Cabinet Offices (but not those of the Ministers) is situated in a quarter of the Forbidden City where once lived the High Officials of the Court. It is both the Elysée and the Matignon, but the entrance is by different doors, according to whether one goes to the one or to the other. The quarter is outside the precincts of the Imperial Palaces, on the banks of an artificial lake which the people of Pekin, with their liking for high-flown language, call the Southern Sea (Nan Hai).

To get to the Prime Minister's, we did not have to pass any security guards or through any formal gateway, but we drove past a factory chimney which here seemed somewhat out of place. I asked the reason for it; it seems it was connected with central heating, a problem of no little difficulty for these old buildings.

After a succession of peaceful courts, bordered with greenery, where several motor cars seemed to be sleeping, we reached the porch where Mr. Chou En-Lai was waiting for us, surrounded by photographers. He wore a pale grey Chinese tunic, and seemed to me younger than his sixty years.

His features were already familiar to us from his many photographs, though I would like to note in this connection that political iconography in China is very much less developed than in the Soviet Union. We knew that he always smiles, even in his formal portraits. His face seems always full of animation, and there is a certain mischievousness, even a mocking air, in his expression. When he wears a cloth cap he looks rather like an artisan.

Mr. Chou En-Lai is a peripatetic communist leader. He was the first of his kind to venture beyond the frontiers of the people's democracies. He broke through the tacit tradition of claustration.

At the first Geneva Conference in 1954 he was the guest of the Swiss and, for a few hours at Berne, the guest of France also. He has visited Djakarta and Karachi, New Delhi and Rangoon.

More recently, he made a tour of the communist countries, including twelve hours in the outskirts of Budapest. It was in January, after his return from this trip, that communist China showed, or at least accentuated, certain tendencies; the launching of the 'rectification' campaign and the speeding up of the 'Hundred Flowers'. . . . (One might assume some relation of cause and effect between this trip and his impressions of it, and these campaigns.)[1] The words attributed to him by the *Jen Min Jih Pao* itself on the occasion of his meeting with Marshal Voroshilov are well known: 'If we do not put an end to our bureaucracy, these children here will tear down the walls of Pekin when they grow up . . . etc.'

Can one say that Mr. Chou En-Lai has ceased to travel even when he does not leave the capital? Pekin is a great crossroads. The Prime Minister and Minister of Foreign Affairs pays the price in his own person. Daily announcements enumerate the receptions that he organizes or honours by his presence. He is always to be seen at them, relaxed, taking a few hours off. He never seems to be overdriven and never seems to be in a hurry.

In China, cocktails (or at least what pass for cocktails by an

[1] The publication of Mao's speech which took place while these notes were being written, will confirm this interpretation by his allusions to Hungary. For these campaigns see Chapter X.

abuse of nomenclature, for I never saw a shaker in the whole country) are usually served between five and half-past seven. They are often served with quite an abundance of dishes, which act as a substitute for the evening meal. It is not the custom to 'put in an appearance' and one does not see the cohorts of new arrivals jostling the withdrawal of those departing. Everyone arrives on one another's heels and leaves in the same way. Mr. Chou En-Lai does not try to avoid the ceremonies with the excuse of his many and heavy duties. He is content to make a profit of ten minutes coming and going. In the meantime, he follows the conversation at his own table for some time and then rises, strolls from group to group, relaxed and laughing freely, yet always watchful. . . .

By such an effort, sustained with an admirable lack of apparent strain, Mr. Chou En-Lai doubtless enhances the prestige of the public relations of the régime. He also continually renews and enriches his living sources of information on the world. He is, as sportsmen would say, always at the top of his form.

Mr. Chou En-Lai is, moreover, a diplomat of the 'sportsman' school. His style is not that of senseless resistance; even if he never says 'yes', he would never run the risk of being nicknamed Mr. No. On the other hand, his is not the style of courteous mystery, the technique of the escape clause and the back reference. He replies with vivacity, he objects, he approves, he contests.

Bismarck liked to say that the best diplomat would be one who always told the truth, for he would never be believed and would mislead all his sparring partners. But in the middle of the twentieth century, the leading diplomats of the world are rarely specialists; they are almost always statesmen, responsible for their actions as well as their words, or likely to be so within a short space of time. Consider the functions of the Secretary of State in America; in England, Eden and Macmillan; in France, Robert Schumann and Mendès-France in 1954; in Italy, Gasperi; and in Germany for so long a time

Adenauer. I am not far from thinking that the duplication of the head of the government and the direction of foreign affairs is the best formula, rather than its duplication with the portfolio of National Economy as I at one time thought. In the Soviet Union, these functions are nominally dissociated; but do we not see them reunited to-day in the person of the First Secretary of the Party? But to return to Mr. Chou En-Lai. I cannot judge if he always tells the truth, like Bismarck's diplomat. But he says many truths and, up to the present, he has gained rather than lost by this.

Our invitation was for a quarter-past one, which is on the late side for a Chinese lunch. But I knew by repute that both Mr. Chou En-Lai and Mr. Mao Tse-Tung are night workers and do not begin their day early. Certainly I would not be the man to blame them for it! In fact, we were to spend another three-quarters of an hour chatting over an aperitif, that is to say, being in China, tea. There were present, besides Mr. Chou En-Lai and ourselves, Mr. and Mrs. Chang Hsi-Jo, and the Assistant Minister of Foreign Affairs, a young man with the air of a 'great revolutionary agent', my neighbour of the previous day and his wife, the Director of Information. There were also the Minister of Foreign Trade, Mr. Yu, and the Secretary-General of the Institute of Foreign Affairs, Mr. Wu Mao-Sun, the perfect example of an Oxford student; an invaluable collaborator for Mr. Chang Hsi-Jo, he is clearly the human link between the parallel diplomacy of the Institute and the official diplomacy of the Prime Minister. I am personally extremely grateful for the ever-smiling and efficient zeal with which he used to organize my trips and carry out my sometimes changeable suggestions. When it so chanced that I was to land at the Western Aerodrome, by a plane unexpectedly in advance of its schedule, Mr. Wu Mao-Sun would always be on the runway to welcome me and enquire about everything. Finally, the last guest, Mr. Tung, the interpreter at important interviews. Mr. Tung is not an interpreter by profession, but a department head at the Foreign Ministry. He had just spent several years in France and there defended a thesis on 'French Policy in the Tai-Ping epoch'.

The first part of our conversation touched on general world political problems. Regarding such problems, the Chinese leaders display a modesty which undoubtedly conceals a well thought out line of policy. They stress that China does not intend to intervene in other people's affairs. She is completely absorbed in the immense effort of her own construction. She has no aspirations to the role of arbitrator or mediator.

For example, while he was listening with close attention to my explanations about Algeria, the Prime Minister seemed all of a sudden uneasy and said to me:

'We can do nothing about this problem. It does not concern us.'

'Most certainly,' I replied, 'and I too do not see it in any other way. But you represent an important factor in world opinion. It would be a good thing that you should be correctly informed.'

Mr. Chou En-Lai then questioned me about the number of French in Algeria, the importance of their holdings there and their place in the country's economy. I insisted on the differences that exist between the Algerian problem on the one hand and the problem of Tunis and Morocco on the other, countries under a Protectorate régime with a legal right to independence judicially laid down, and whose peoples did not benefit by any form of participation in the political life of France. I pointed out to him the very liberal policies that had been followed with regard to those countries and which I had some reason to know well. I was very pleased at his reply:

'I fully understand', he told me, 'that the problem of Algeria is not the same as that of Morocco and Tunis, but I think that you ought to find the solution by negotiation.'

We could hardly fail to touch on other thorny problems, such as the Suez affair. Mr. Chou En-Lai had the advantage over me of having known Colonel Nasser personally. He first saw him at the Bandung Conference, and then at Djakarta. I recalled, moreover, that according to the reports at the time, the Egyptian dictator was classed as a 'moderate'.

We knew the points where our views could not coincide. Mr. Chou En-Lai, like the other Chinese leaders, avoids involving himself in contradictions. He takes up the points in the discussion which he approves; others are not mentioned. The zone of silence masks that of deadlock.

Whether for this reason or some other, I noted that Chou En-Lai, as later also Mao Tse-Tung, avoided any opinion on the Hungarian affair.

But the conversation always returned to the subject of peace. China is passionately devoted to peace, for what other country, eager to make up for such immense backwardness by a superhuman effort, has such need of peace? For this reason she desires the success of every enterprise, every initiative, which aims at relaxation of tension, at conciliation, at disarmament.

Mr. Chou En-Lai takes an interest in all the various plans for disarmament, but as an observer, with the reserve of a state not represented in the qualified organizations. He asked for an explanation of a point in my plan, already put forward at Geneva, which consisted in linking reductions in military expenditure with aid to underdeveloped countries.

While trying to avoid the wearisome insistence of an originator, it has always seemed to me that no other procedure exists that is able to assure at one and the same time control and sanctions, whereas my plan completely assures both. If a country has taken upon itself to reduce its military expenditure by a hundred milliards and if these hundred milliards must be earmarked, under one of the various forms implied by economic transfer, for a special fund, how can this be falsified? This would mean to inflict automatically upon oneself a fine of the same amount, which would be liable to indefinite extension from one year to another. It would inevitably mean undermining one's currency as well as dishonouring one's signature. What other form of control is possible? Can one count the rifles in their racks, the uniforms in the quartermasters' stores, verify an ever-shifting potential?

From another point of view, conversion of sterile into active credits has the merit of transforming a negative into a positive problem, and giving activities leading to disarmament a foundation other than physical fear — the glow of life and faith in the future. Naturally, in this system of 'control become co-operation', the contributing states could also be beneficiaries as far as their own underdeveloped regions were concerned.

But Mr. Chou En-Lai had certain misgivings about the organization and application of the proposed fund. He feared some enterprise under American control.

'There could be no question of that. The essential idea is that of co-management between the contracting parties. Surely that would be a chance for the two hostile blocs to come closer together in constructive work and to bring into the open the pacific rivalry of the differing forms of economy in all the fullness of the greatest human task of present times, a task which China is in a better position than any other nation to appreciate?'

I thought that my explanations reassured Mr. Chou En-Lai on that point. But I would not like to swear that they convinced him. I was pleased, none the less, to have had the chance of putting my plan before him. Since the Chinese know how to wait, I believe that they also know how to reflect. On this problem of disarmament, Mr. Chou En-Lai is above all interested by anything that might rapidly be put into practice.

'Our needs are immense. Our construction cannot wait. Whatever happens, we are diminishing our expenditure on armaments every year and we intend to go on doing so.'

At another point in the conversation when I alluded jokingly to the dust which smothers everything in Pekin, he took up once again the great Chinese theme:

'That is nature. When peace is guaranteed, we shall be able to devote all our energies to reforming nature.'

We took our seats.

During lunch, the conversation touched on the most varied and personal subjects. While teaching me how to roll in a pancake, the inevitable glazed duck garnished with onion, and serving me with red sugared Chinese wine in a slender glass, Mr. Chou En-Lai recalled his stay in France between 1924 and 1927. He had worked there as a student and also as a manual worker, in Paris and Rouen.

He obviously understood French, though I never heard him say more than a few words. But during our meeting with Mao Tse-Tung his knowledge was to become more apparent.

'It was while I was amongst you,' he explained, 'that I was converted to communism. I observed, I shared the life of my fellow-workers and I came to the conclusion that it was not possible to transform the wage earners into capitalists, but that it was possible to transform the capitalists into wage earners.'

He made this remark as a jest; yet, none the less, is it not exactly what has been done here in seven years?

I had naturally some arguments to put forward; the already advanced social structure of France in 1927 and the great progress made since, with the reasons which might justify a reverse transformation.

Naturally, too, he concluded: 'Conditions differ in every country. Each people must choose its own economic régime.'

It was towards the end of the dessert and during the hour that followed that we got to the main subject, on which the Prime Minister intended to enlighten me fully. That was the international position of China and particularly, since this concerned me most directly, her relations with France. It was the same subject that I had touched upon the day before at the dinner of the Institute for Foreign Affairs.

The Franco-Chinese paradox might seem even more surprising than certain others. It was now almost three years since the French Prime Minister with all his ministers had entrained at the Gare de Lyon to entertain the Chinese 'premier' to lunch at the French Embassy in Berne. That very same day I found myself, in the interim, head of the French Government while the French Republic and the People's Democratic Republic of China, still officially ignoring each other's existence, met in the Swiss capital. They still ignore one another! At that time it seemed that the situation must very soon be normal. Yet, between the Berne lunch and the Pekin lunch, not a move has been made.

The day before I had had occasion to point out that the question of diplomatic recognition was not an isolated one. At a pinch it could be so regarded by France, but not by China. The opinion of Mr. Chou En-Lai echoed my own view and justified it beyond any manner of doubt.

If nothing more were involved than the question of recognition, China would doubtless see nothing but advantage to be obtained and would naturally feel nothing but bitterness for the defaulting states. But the question is quite another thing. It forms part of a diplomatic complex, together with that of representation in the United Nations, and with the question of Formosa.

For China, the main question, or to be more exact the key question, is Formosa.

The main headache of the Chinese leaders is to avoid the 'second China', to reject every plan, to frustrate every manoeuvre intended to perpetuate the existence of 'two Chinas', the China of Pekin and the China of Taipeh.

The Chinese suppose, rightly or wrongly, that the Americans are preparing some withdrawal tactic which would take this form. It is this that they fear more than anything else.

The People's China cannot conceive being put on a similar footing with Formosa; she cannot consider recognition concurrently with Formosa. She will never agree to take part in a parallel system, to share plenipotentiaries or accept credentials drawn up for both Chinas.

Rather than find herself 'paired' with Taipeh in some sort of diplomatic mesh, Pekin much prefers the *status quo* from which, after all, she in no way suffers.

'When the Formosan refugees understand that there will be no second China, then the problem will not be far from solution.'

What then can France do? Without doubt if she reversed the situation and broke all her links with Formosa, China would only be able to welcome this initiative with gratitude. But, here in Pekin, no one thinks that we could go as far as that. No one asks it of us.

The Chinese are well aware of what we could reasonably do, though not without taking certain risks. To propose to send an ambassador to Pekin and, none the less, to keep a chargé d'affaires in Formosa, to discuss temporary expedients in the United Nations. . . . But what we can reasonably do does not interest them; on the other hand it makes them uneasy. It would be a breach in the system of 'all or nothing' which they evidently prefer, since they know that by sticking to it they will one day get everything.

Therefore until France goes as far as an extreme decision, which is scarcely conceivable, Mr. Chou En-Lai believes that recognition would not only be useless but would, in fact, be an unfriendly gesture.

Is it necessary to say any more? Should one not go so far as to think that China does not want the *status quo* to come to an end — even in the form most honourable to her — within the limited relations of a single country? Does not China find it to her advantage to be placed in the most absurd position possible in regard to as much of the world as possible, until she receives her '*restitutio in integrum*'?

In any case, they do not want us to remain in expectancy. It is quite the contrary that is suggested to us.

'That should not hinder us,' Mr. Chou En-Lai underlined,

'from developing our other relations — notably to take up again what you have started in economic affairs' — and he took to witness Mr. Yu, Minister of Foreign Trade — 'and at the same time to develop cultural exchanges.'

I asked Mr. Chou En-Lai if he were still thinking of an amicable settlement with Chiang Kai-Shek.

'There is not yet any direct contact on this matter,' he replied, 'but it is not out of the question.'

Mention of the Formosa question led me to refer in passing to Hong Kong.

'That is not the same thing. There has been a treaty about Hong Kong, which creates a special situation. I do not say the same as far as the New Territories are concerned.'

Finally, on the subject of the United Nations, the Prime Minister, in conformance with his doctrine, did not envisage any concession. He refused to make the slightest distinction between admission to that organization and the seat of Permanent Member of the Security Council.

These two questions were one.

It was clear to see that the Chinese modesty which I referred to above does not involve humility.

Settlement on Formosa, diplomatic recognition, return to the United Nations, the Security Council, 'the Big Five', international prestige, Asiatic leadership — all these interlock. The whole mechanism must work smoothly and accurately. The essential point is that one alone should set in action all the others. The whole operation must work without a hitch. Care must be taken lest the least grain of sand get into the works, such as a clumsy and premature recognition, even if well intentioned. Above all, there must not be, there must not be even a hint of, a second China!

Certain foreign observers, and not unimportant ones at that, think that China does not really want to see these problems solved; for example, that she does not want to take her place in the United Nations. They believe that she will be in no hurry to assume her responsibilities and that it pleases her to continue to play the role of martyr.

I cannot in any way accept this interpretation.

The Chinese are sure of their aims and are firmly convinced of them.

They are in no hurry, because they do not want to take risks.

Mr. Chou En-Lai made use on several occasions of the phrases: 'We can wait', 'The Chinese know how to wait.'

Who will gainsay him?

This quality is traditional with the Chinese people. It is not for nothing that the emblematic tortoise, through all the lands of China, supports the stone monuments of a fabled past. . . .

Only it is strange to hear this maxim so frequently affirmed by a Chinese, who is the most swift, the most vivacious, the least 'oriental philosopher and fatalist', that one could hope to meet.

One might well ask, also, whether in these past few years this genius for 'long patience' has not given place, as Valéry would say, to the genius of 'long impatience'.

The Chinese know how to wait.

They know too what they are waiting for.

Knowing exactly what is their aim, having determined their way of achieving it, their waiting is an active waiting which makes time work for them.

I wonder if we in the west could say as much. Do we know, exactly, what we are waiting for in this matter? Can we say that, during these past few years, time has worked for us? Can we say that we see ourselves daily getting nearer to an aim of which, furthermore, we are unaware?

Also I am not wholly convinced by the proofs that I have sought to bring. Let us be clear; I am convinced of the existence of these proofs, of their existence from the Chinese point of view. I can believe them to be sincere and even find them reasonable and clever.

But I am in no way convinced that we must stop at this

point, that we must not look for other things, and take refuge, as we have been urged to do, in a policy of wait and see.

France must, first of all, make every effort to regain the initiative — her present eclipse on the great world political scene can only be temporary — and, more especially, to set the course of the west towards a happier approach to the Chinese problem; I shall return to this point later.

But in our own sphere if it should happen that the general evolution of affairs continues to hang fire, why should we not consider for once taking the initiative?

It might be said that, as in marriage, it takes two to agree. Could one not say also that it takes two to disagree?

Without doubt there can be no question of placing before the government of the People's China proposals that will meet with a rebuff. But we can take them at their word. Since what they fear is a second China, and since we on our side have no reason to approve the co-existence of two Chinas, there is nothing to prevent us from renewing our diplomatic relations at Pekin with China — which is at Pekin — while leaving a reduced staff on the island territory of Formosa in the form of a consular representation which is all that it deserves. If we hold ourselves always ready for such a decision, that could only increase our prestige in the west and favour a total settlement. If, however, we were induced to act in isolation, I think that no one could blame us for this attitude; not the Chinese, even if it went counter to their final ideas and calculations, for it is not our place to submit to the subtleties of their manoeuvres, but only to take account of explicit and legitimate claims; nor the English, since they are, at this very moment, in just such a situation; nor, finally, the Americans, since we would be merely following the example of the English. No one could accuse us of breaking the unity of friendship. The Americans themselves would, I am sure, not be backward in gratitude for having helped them to get out of an impasse. They have often enough and, in my view, more than once rightly, given us lessons in realism.

But we have no pretensions of paying them back in their own coin. There is no reason whatsoever why a lesson should suddenly lose its value from the simple fact that the East which is in question is no longer the Middle East but the Far East.

CHAPTER III

THE GREAT WALL AND THE LONG MARCH

Meeting with President Mao Tse-Tung

AUDIENCES with President Mao Tse-Tung are preceded by successive warnings which reminded me of summons to the Elysée during ministerial crises. On Wednesday evening, Mr. Wu Mao-Sun, who invited us out to dine, told me that the President would certainly receive me the following day. I at once asked if it would not be more suitable to forgo the excursion to the Great Wall which we were due to make during the day. My fellow guests were frankly amused. There was no likelihood that the President would think of receiving me in the morning, or even in the afternoon. He is a man of the evening. I did not, therefore, risk the mishap of Frank Harris who had been summoned by President Kruger at six o'clock in the morning.

This point settled, it seemed to me particularly opportune to start a day which was due to end with such an interview by a visit to the Great Wall. So we set out for Pataling, about forty-five miles from Pekin on a bad road and almost smothered by dust, even with only one window half open. On the outskirts of the city we still came across lorries, but soon all that were to be seen were country waggons fitted with rubber tyres and drawn sometimes by horses but more often by donkeys. These slow carts with their sleepy drivers made us think of the more remote country districts of France, but these were not agricultural vehicles pitching their way towards some neighbouring farm. For the most part they were carrying building materials, bricks or pipes. The products of the soil remained at an earlier stage of transportation, the donkey without the cart.

Pataling is a little railway station, lost in the narrow and picturesque zone of the mountains which separates two expanses of plain. One reaches it by way of a beetling ravine where cyclopean walls break through stretches of thick undergrowth. The Wall itself, which seems quite new, follows its irregular contours, giving the impression of a zigzag design and even of separate sections. The way leads up a winding road with sharply inclined planes and steep stairways, leading up to one or the other of the watchtowers, whence the two plains can again be seen and, to the north, an immense lake reservoir. But the biting wind discouraged reverie.

'We have marched twenty thousand li,'[1] said Mao in one of his poems, 'yet only those can call themselves men who have reached the foot of the Great Wall.'

On our return to the hotel, about five in the afternoon, we received confirmation of the audience arranged for the same evening. Our companions were much excited by the fact. To avoid any inadequacy, it was at once decided that the dinner arranged for that evening, and which was to have been held outside the hotel, would take place in the hotel itself. At dinner we again met Mr. Lo Ta-Kang, an excellent French interpreter, and his wife, also a French teacher. Mr. and Mrs. Lo Ta-Kang had lived for a long time in Montparnasse. They were devoted heart and soul to the régime, which allows Mr. Lo Ta-Kang to free himself from his teaching duties and devote himself to the adaptation of our great authors to Chinese.

At nine o'clock, Mr. Chia made a formal appearance in the little dining-room to ask us to be ready at ten minutes to ten. At the appointed time, in the hall, Mr. Wu Mao-Sun kept glancing at his wrist-watch and said we were to be ready within a few minutes. I was shortly to understand the reason for the exactitude of this time-keeping.

[1] More than 6,250 miles.

We entered the presidential quarter once again, this time passing under a fine red gateway, the Gateway of the New China, as it is in fact always called. I saw only two sentries.

The car followed an avenue bordered by willows along the Southern Sea.

A little Chinese courtyard, two Judas trees and some hawthorn in full flower . . . then the President stepped forward to meet us at the foot of the steps and I was surprised to find myself suddenly quite close to him. I then understood the exactness of the time-keeping, which enabled him to show this delicate mark of courtesy.

In appearance Mao Tse-Tung seemed not so young, not so full-faced, not quite so supple as in his current photographs. He is powerful in build with a vigorous bearing (at the age of sixty-three he swam the Yang Tse Kiang at a point where it is more than twelve miles across).[1] His manners are of extreme and pleasing simplicity.

I think with amusement whilst I am writing these lines, that a few days ago a leading columnist described Mao as an old, decrepit man, ravaged by some mysterious disease and virtually disinterested in public affairs.

Half little palace, half bungalow, we entered a fairly large hall lit by neon floods and Chinese lanterns, with ornaments in carved wood reaching down from the ceiling. On one side was a conference table covered with a red cloth; on the other, a circle of armchairs where we sat. The Prime Minister, Mr. Chou En-Lai, was there, as also Mr. Chang Hsi-Jo, Mr. Wu Mao-Sun and, naturally, Mr. Tung. On the side-tables tea was served in beautiful porcelain tea-pots decorated only by a number in blue ideograms. It was not the usual jasmine tea, but a long-leaf tea from Hangchow.

'You are quite a small delegation,' said Mao laughingly. 'With only two persons it is easier to agree.'

[1] This performance has since been 'rectified' by the newspapers to the figure of a little over six miles which is, none the less, still a remarkable feat. It was after this exploit that Mao composed the second poem about the Serpent and the Tortoise.

Then he went out of his way to thank me in his turn for having received the Chinese Youth delegation.

By comparison with the Head of State, the Prime Minister, Chou En-Lai, seemed more slyly mischievous than ever. He was clearly amused at being able to understand what I was saying before anyone else did, and he kept a sharp watch for slips in Mr. Tung's translation, in order to correct them. He had the advantage of knowing my subjects of conversation beforehand and he helped me to explain certain of my points of view, while making it quite clear that he did not share them.

The President Mao Tse-Tung spoke of China with a restrained passion, an expression of despondency mingled with confidence.

'You have seen for yourself what sort of state the country is in, and how backward we are. The task is immense.'

I alluded to the progress already made.

'Yes, without doubt, but it is very little in comparison.... There is so much to be done!'

He bowed his head a little as if under the weight of too heavy a destiny. He joined his two hands together. It has been said of Mao Tse-Tung that there is something in him of the soldier and the peasant, but I find that he has more the gestures of a man of religion; he makes one think of the Chief of a religious community, preferably at the time of the Military Orders.

I remarked that Chinese communism had benefited from his absence of dogmatism; could there not be a future for some of his supple formulas, for example that of the mixed economy?

'That is perhaps no more than a stage, a transition. Our aim is total socialism.'

The President, who takes much interest in agrarian economics, asked for the French system of co-operatives by products to be explained to him. I stressed the excellent results attained. He shook his head; approval and denial at the same time.

'It would not be possible here. The holdings are too small.

The peasant cannot divide his interests between co-operative exploitation and personal exploitation.'

What can be expected from the '*cheng-feng*', the 'Hundred Flowers and the Hundred Schools'? I told the President of the intense interest that we had in these campaigns which might be held to show — though from a very different angle — a 'liberalizing' tendency.[1]

'Yes, criticism must be allowed. If not, centres of irritation and incomprehension are created. Men must be allowed to say what they have in their hearts.'

He confirmed that the two movements are linked, and that they are inspired by a similar tendency.

But: 'One must take account of special conditions. With a people like this it is necessary to observe certain limits.'

The comments and the tone of the President on this matter confirmed me in the view that I had already formed. Certainly, these two campaigns are not a negligible matter, but it would be a great mistake to see in them a major turning point from the western angle. We have not gone beyond the varying limits allowed by the communist régimes. Moreover we are coming once again towards the middle line which has always been that of Mao Tse-Tung; careful handling of the non-communists, the incorporation of different sectors of the country's life into the régime, and education of the communists themselves in order to make them understand these aims.

The President mentioned once more the term 'brain-washing', which does not have the pejorative sense here that we attribute to it in the west. It indicates, however, that if the present campaigns are educational for the communists themselves, it is for the others — those whom one might call the virtual opposition — that they are really 'curative'.

It is mainly a question of making those who are discontented

[1] At the time of the interview, the speech of February had not yet been made public. See the chapter on 'The Political Campaigns', Chapter X.

express their discontent, of bringing their reticences into the open.

That is already considered to be a result in itself, to be a good treatment for the patients. Also, it amounts to a sorting out, to distinguish in these discontents and reticences all that is legitimate or merely admissible, even if very violently expressed. On the contrary, whenever a real deviation may appear, even if expressed in a very moderate form — an external contradiction — it can be foreseen that it will thus be easily localized and, by means of the counter-offensive which has already been set in motion, vigorously reduced.[1]

Recent events in foreign policy provided Mao Tse-Tung with a theme for one of those allegories of which he is so fond.

'We have a story in China about a heron and a mussel. The heron picked up the mussel on a beach, but the mussel closed itself on the heron's beak. A long argument began between them. In three days, said the mussel to the heron, you will be dead. You too, said the heron to the mussel, will be dead in three days for lack of water. Neither would give way and, in the meantime, a fisherman passed by and captured both of them.'

'Was it a Russian or an American fisherman?'

The expected reply came with a smile:

'In my view, it was more likely an American fisherman.' It is the Americans who make China uneasy.

'Why do they need bases so close to our territory? We have no Chinese bases near the American continent.'

'Do you really believe that the Americans are thinking of war?'

'The American people most certainly do not want war.'

'Nor do their leaders,' I said. I told him that during the week of the Geneva Conference in 1955, seeing President

[1] I must recall that the account of this interview was written before the launching of the campaign against the right-wing deviationists. It seems to me that later events have confirmed my impressions.

Eisenhower every day, I had been able to convince myself of his profound desire for peace. Since the Chinese leaders had been gracious enough to recognize my personal efforts in favour of a slackening of international tension, I asked them to take note of this evidence too.

I added that if the policy of détente, which had made some progress, had since seemed to be blocked, I saw the cause for this in events for which the western leaders could in no way be blamed. I tried to make him understand the emotion, the feelings of repugnance, of the French people after the events in Hungary. This reflection seemed to touch the President on the raw.

'Would you say,' he asked me at once, 'that the French people would feel any bitterness against China because of these events?'

'Certainly not. China was not involved. But there is a tendency to think in terms of blocs; the policy of the blocs, the "communist bloc".'

'China', affirmed Mao Tse-Tung, 'is an independent state. She is absolutely independent of the Soviet Union. If we have asked for experts and machinery from the Soviet Union, it is because we have need of them. We cannot do without them. But the men who have come will go away again once their work is finished. And we shall pay for all that we have taken.'

Without doubt 'China, being a communist state, feels herself in sympathy with the Soviet Union.' But the President rejected the idea of a 'communist bloc'.

'You did not come to an understanding with Nasser,' he remarked, 'and yet he is not a socialist. What are you afraid of, then? Only a quarter of humanity is socialist. There remains three-quarters, including states like India, in which to apply your economic system. Competition and comparison can be carried out in peace.'

We agreed that we should not despair of the future. The President, Mao Tse-Tung, recalled, in passing, my attitude towards the ban on nuclear tests, and I took up once more, in a duet with Mr. Chou En-Lai, an explanation of my plan for disarmament by transfer.[1]

'France', said Mao Tse-Tung, 'can again play a role of reconciliation, of mediation. . . . France has had a glorious history. She must surmount her present difficulties. She is more qualified than China for such a role, which belongs to her rather than to us.'

Once again that Chinese modesty, tinged with courtesy yet full of pride. It is because China has made such staggering progress that she can insist on her 'insufficiencies', her backwardness, her archaism.

Before taking our leave, we talked to the President about his poems.

'That is an old story. Once I composed poems, it is true. That was when I lived in the saddle. On horseback, one has the time. One can search out rhymes and rhythms; one can reflect. It was good, that life on horseback. Sometimes, these days, I look back on it with regret.'

Last April Mao Tse-Tung authorized the Chinese review *Poetry* to publish a series of sixteen poems in the classical style. He did not do so without hesitation, for he had made use of very ancient forms of prosody. Was he not running the risk of encouraging youth to follow the errors of the past? But one of these poems is dated 1956. . . .

Poetry is not a mere anecdote in the biography of Mao Tse-Tung. I believe, indeed, that it is one of the keys to his personality. Mao is not, like so many Marxists, a man of one book. In these short pieces, his thought is freed from the jargon of the party and the claptrap of dialectics. Themes of the revolution are presented in simple form, vivid and profound, accessible to all the men of this country — and to the men of all time.

There is something of the humanist in this revolutionary.

[1] See preceding chapter and post-scriptum.

That alone is enough to explain certain original aspects of Chinese communism.

The President accompanied us to our cars. He took me by the arm and pointed out a step in the darkness. From this last picture of him through the car windows — the well-known face above the close shut collar of the beige tunic — that hand raised in a gesture of sympathy — I retain an impression of force, of naturalness and of 'presence'.

And I thought, while driving farther and farther away along the shore of the Southern Sea, about the incredible paradox that this Head of State is not recognized as such by a great number of powers.

Juridically and diplomatically, for a great part of the west, Mao Tse-Tung and the China of Mao Tse-Tung do not exist!

Is there, however, any other statesman who governs so populous a country? Is there anyone, wherever he may be, who governs with greater power? Is there a single one of them to-day, or for that matter were there ever many such, who identifies himself to such an extent with a nation and with a people, in the whole course of history?

What advantage is it to us to disregard so evident and so formidable a reality? So I once again repeat the question that was in my mind at the close of my meeting with Chou En-Lai; what exactly are we waiting for?

What aims does western diplomacy, in any case divided, propose?

Can anyone seriously believe in the fiction of 'the other China'? Can anyone still believe in the fantastic hypothesis of the return of Chiang Kai-Shek and the Kuo Min Tang?

Even more, can we seriously support the hypothesis of 'the two Chinas'?

It is not by mingling the world of phantasmagoria and the world of reality that we can bring to birth an intermediate world where living beings and phantasms consort in a composite existence. What is fictitious does not thereby become more real; what is real does not thereby become fictitious.

Can we really think that the policy of embargo will hinder the economic development of China? Such an idea would not, in fact, be very magnanimous. It would, in any event, be a chimaera.

Can we really believe that we are making the Chinese more inclined to a liberal economy by preventing them from becoming acquainted with it, and presenting it to them in the guise of an enemy?

Can we think that we will ever succeed in withdrawing the Chinese from Soviet influence by obliging them to ask from the Soviet Union, as Mao Tse-Tung reminded me, for products and services that are absolutely indispensable to them?

The challenge to pacific competition between the different economic systems has been launched by men whom I believe to be sincere. Why not accept it?

The game must be played, the markets left wide open, competition not only accepted, but proposed. The free economies throughout the world already have a strong dose of socialism. As the standard of life of the most backward peoples is raised, will not socialism feel the need of a greater freedom?

We have wanted, in our turn, to build a wall around China, but it is ourselves whom we are shutting out. This attitude might have had its justification at the start, by the force of circumstances and the reaction of feelings. But now?

Have we lost the sense of movement?

Are we going to remain as immovable as the rocks, while other rocks are breaking up around us?

Faced with the new China, are we to become the unforeseen disciples of those Emperors who reigned two thousand years ago?

Are we to oppose the men of the Long March with the strategy and diplomacy of the Great Wall?

CHAPTER IV

THE RUSSIANS AND THE CHINESE—KHRUSHCHEV AND MAO

ARE PARALLEL biographies in the manner of Plutarch likely to return to fashion? As, among contemporary non-communist politicians, I have had the comparatively rare privilege, though it may be through no great merit of my own, to know both the Soviet and the Chinese leaders, I have often been asked for a comparison of the personalities of Mao Tse-Tung and Khrushchev — the two men who are the leaders of a third of humanity and who could, at the drop of a hat, throw into the balance the 'little milliard' of the communist world. At first sight, it is the differences between these two men which are the most striking; Mao is notable for his serenity of manner and language. He speaks slowly in short, compact sentences, taking a moment for reflection between each. Nikita Khrushchev, on the contrary, is blunt and full of life, gives free rein to his thoughts in immediate and extreme expression, more liable to exaggeration than to taciturnity. He can scarcely be imagined passing his leisure moments in the learned and harmonious exercise of classical prosody and I would not say of him as I have said of Mao that he makes one think of a man of religion — even though it happens that he sometimes speaks of God. (My master, Paul Boyer, liked to say that one must know the Gospels to be able to understand the deliberations of a Soviet.) None the less, there are points of similarity between the imperturbable horseman of the Long March and the ebullient First Secretary of the Soviet Communist Party. First of all, their common liking for fable and folk metaphor is not an anecdotic chance. It is the sign of an inclination towards popular taste, of an intelligence that seeks to meet the reasoning of the simplest of men in order to make themselves understood by them. The two men express themselves in a very different way, but they usually do so in a simple, clear and direct manner. The outbursts and even the excesses of Khrushchev thus tend to the same result and doubtless with the same aim as the careful and measured parsimony of Mao Tse-Tung; to explain and to impose conclusions and instructions that are immediately assimilable.

Both men are to some extent of peasant origin, rooted in the soil, and they have always shown their care for the men and things of the soil. Mao, it is well known, made a success of the Chinese revolution by turning to the peasant masses, interesting them and enlisting them in his cause. Khrushchev, for his part, has not carried out an agrarian reform, since it was no longer to be made in Russia, but his great enterprise, his chosen task, 'his thesis', is an agricultural enterprise; the reclamation of the virgin lands.

Both have a long record as militant communists — and they have remained militants, taking an interest in other militants, receiving them and listening to them. They search even more widely for human contacts. They are not like Stalin or even like Molotov, men of the ivory tower. Mao loves to make unheralded visits to collectives; he is quite likely to appear unexpectedly in a barracks. When he was going to swim the Yang Tse Kiang, they gathered beforehand a team of young worker sportsmen and told them that an important person was coming to take his exercise in their company, and only at the last moment did they learn that their companion was no other than Mao himself. More recently, he paid a visit to the capitalist circles of Shanghai.

Khrushchev too loves to move about and see people. One of his recently expressed criticisms of Stalin dealt with his systematic isolation and his distrust of direct information. When I visited the virgin lands in the Koustamai district of

Kazakstan, I was taken around by the *predoblispolkom* (the President of the Executive Council of the district, the principal personage in the area, a sort of Prefect and presiding Chairman in one), Mr. Batamirov, a man of strong build and vigorous personality. Mr. Batamirov frequently spoke to me of the visit Mr. Khrushchev had made to the same district, taking an interest in the methods of cultivation, criticizing the construction of the new houses in the villages, etc.

Introducing me to the President of the Kolkhoz, Mr. Batamirov said with a great horse laugh: 'This is the man who tricked Nikita Sergeivitch Khrushchev. He told him that the yield of the harvest would be about twenty-five quintals, whereas it was over thirty!'

The traits common to Khrushchev and Mao reveal a similar disposition and must logically lead them along similar paths. Mindful of the opinions of others, they do not display that 'contempt of the masses' which is the great temptation of communist leaders of the Stalin type. We have noted, at the inception of the 'rectification' campaigns, Mao's warning against this contempt of the masses and against taking up the attitude of the 'mandarins'.

In the Soviet Union, during the campaign against Molotov and other 'fractionalists', a certain expression '*barski*' was frequently employed; it means feudal, 'in the manner of a feudal landlord'. The four anti-party men were accused of having 'feudally' disregarded, on this or that point, both the interests and the opinions of the people.

From the moment that leaders like Khrushchev and Mao (whatever share the liking for personal popularity may have in this attitude) take the opinions and the interests of the masses seriously, they must in the normal course of events try to satisfy them and pursue a policy of well-being and improvement of living standards. This is what, in his picturesque phrase, Khrushchev calls 'buttered Leninism'.

For the same reason, in international affairs, these statesmen must logically be anxious for a policy of relaxation, even were it only to be able to reduce unproductive commitments and increase those available for consumer goods.

I think then, sentiments and theories aside, that those tendencies which in the communist world are concerned with improving living standards must, in external affairs, be conciliatory tendencies.

Undoubtedly that does not mean to say that we, merely because of that, have any guarantees. Certain attitudes and certain decisions may give a quite contrary impression. The consciousness of means with these leaders cannot be as clear as consciousness of aims — and that too may become obscured. None the less, the logic of the situation is irrefutable. There is the trend, which one might call Stalinist, that of the man immured in the Kremlin, like the podestà of Florence during his term of office, shut up in his tower and taking his meals in solitude, the trend of the communist 'seigneur', the 'bureaucrat' or 'mandarin' who, in internal affairs, refuses to pay any heed to currents of opinion and the living standards of the people and who, in external affairs, refuses all contacts as enervating and dangerous. There is, on the other hand, the trend which seeks a certain amount of popular support, which aims at improving living standards — and which, in external affairs, tries to organize co-existence even if that means maintaining imperialist, expansionist or merely propagandist viewpoints.

The external policy of the leaders can no doubt be determined to a certain degree by sentiments or ideas directly applied to this aim; but it essentially depends on their internal policy and, even more so, on what I will call their 'code of conduct'.

In all events and, of course, without relaxing our vigilance for a single instant, it is infinitely preferable for the West that the communist world should be governed by men like Mao and Khrushchev than by communists of the Stalinist type, be they Russians or Chinese.

Thus we must, I repeat, without it leading us into dangerous concessions or without compensating advantages, do all that is in our power to help non-Stalinist trends in the communist world.

In this connection I recall a significant exchange of views which I had shortly after the vote on the Paris Agreements with a Soviet personality, whose pro-French views were well known to me.

'We must', I explained, 'give credit to Germans like Adenauer. We must support a pacific and renovated Germany as against the Germany of Hitler.'

'Then you must', he replied, 'apply similar reasoning to Russia. You must aid by your attitude those men who, in our country, are playing the cards of comprehension and of peace. Their task is often a hard one. If you meet their approaches with rebuffs, and if their endeavours result only in checks and disorder, they are compromised and the others can sweep them away.'

CHAPTER V

CONVERSATIONS WITH MR. L. W. M.

AMONG those Chinese who, whether officials or not, have their place 'in the régime', there are some who show a certain independence of spirit. They enlarge upon the usual themes, but they avoid the use of simple statement, make reservations or criticisms and allow for shades of meaning. They strive to explain its phenomena in a manner comprehensible to western ideas.

It was after a synthesis of a number of different conversations that I created, for my own satisfaction and convenience, an imaginary Chinese personage whom I will call, with your permission, by the initials L. W. M.

Here are certain typical instances of the moods of Mr. L. W. M.

If I ask him:

'Are you a Marxist?'

He replies:

'Yes, I am a Marxist.'

But if one goes more deeply into the matter, he adds:

'But I willingly agree that there are some parts of Marxism that are out of date to-day.'

If I mention the subject, the most delicate of all, of the events in Hungary — the officials insist on supporting the Soviet viewpoint, though many avoid discussing it at all — Mr. L. W. M. declares:

'At the moment we subscribe to the Soviet interpretation, but I admit that here we are not fully informed.'

In replies such as these everyone who is accustomed to discussions with Russian or Chinese communists will admit that if there is conformity in Mr. L. W. M., there is also independence.

And when I am about to leave, Mr. L. W. M. will say to me with an expression which there is no mistaking:

'I beg you. We count on you. Try to obtain an improvement in our relations. We intellectuals have a physical need to refresh ourselves by contacts with the West.'

After all my interviews with illustrious personages I would now like to record a conversation of a general nature with this Chinese, whose fictional character guarantees his reasonableness and whose orthodoxy does not go so far as repeating parrot phrases. But, on the whole he acts — as you will see — as an intelligent advocate for the régime.

The Conditions of Communism in China

'Never forget', said Mr. L. W. M., 'that the communist régime has not brought to us here only the communist system such as you define it by the manner of government and the structure of its economy. It is not for that reason alone that it is followed and not for that reason alone that it is to be judged.

'Communism, so often described as international, is here primarily national. The Chinese communists were, originally, the best and most efficient nationalists. For that reason many nationalists who were not communists and who very often have not since become communists, joined them. There has been a subordination of the nationalists to communist leadership.

'The régime has brought to us independence, unity and order.

'We were previously the humiliated and the injured. The memory of even the oldest of living Chinese cannot recall before 1949 the picture of a united, free and respected country.

'The China which we have known was always partially occupied, territorially divided, "protected" by foreign powers and often in dispute among her protectors.'

'But surely national feeling also played its part in 1917 at the time of the Soviet October Revolution and subsequently?'

'Undoubtedly, but not to the same extent as in China. The Empire of the Tsars had known the humiliation of military defeat, but the international situation of Russia, her existence as a nation, was in no way comparable to the disintegration of China. Then again Bolshevism was itself born in humiliation; without doubt it was humiliation resulting from the disorder and the tsarist defeats, but it is none the less true that it was born in humiliation. Its first act was to ratify this humiliation and defeat. Chinese communism was spared the humiliation of a Brest-Litovsk: but what am I saying? On the contrary it asserted itself as a reaction, a revenge and established its prestige.'

In China national interest supports the régime, doubtless even more than in Russia. This creates a situation precisely the opposite to that which exists in the so-called 'satellites' of Central Europe. It is as difficult to find a national opposition to communism in China as it is difficult to find a national support for communism in Poland or in Hungary.[1]

'Then there is also internal order. This is part and parcel of the idea of independence and unity. Together they create the feeling of national pride. One appreciates order in a different way when one has more or less been deprived of it.

'I speak of order in every sense of the word.

'Firstly financial order, monetary stability: it is a paradox that it is communism which, alone, has been able to bring to its sworn enemies, the business men, the very bread of capitalism: money.

'I speak too of order in the streets, of personal security. We have preserved a bitter memory of secret societies, of factions which imposed levies and ransoms, recruited bullies and gangsters.

'And that veritable theft that was usury?

[1] The passages in italics represent the reflections of the author.

'Add hygiene in everyday life, those campaigns that have been so jeered at, the communists armed with fly-swatters, the moral and material elimination of filth. . . .

'I will only mention in passing the development of emancipation within the family, for that evolution had already commenced after the First World War. None the less, the régime has markedly speeded up the process.'

'All these benefits, which are incontestable, are not necessarily connected with Marxist doctrine. Could not a non-Marxist régime have been able to procure them for you?'

'Without doubt, in theory. In practice, I do not think so. The Kuo Min Tang missed the boat.'

The weeds had grown so fast that the soil had to be burnt to destroy the roots. Revolution was necessary, not evolution. But the spirit of the democratic revolution had been broken, it had run into shoal water. Only the Marxist revolution could, therefore, obtain this 'radical' result.

I must intervene to say that I have asked the same question of many people, particularly to declared opponents of the régime: Europeans who knew China very well, who were still living there or who had lived there. I did not find any difference of opinion. At the first stop on my journey, an observer like Mr. Suhrawardy, a confirmed anti-communist, had given me the same reply.

Not one of them thought that any other régime would have been able to carry out in this lapse of time, or even over a much longer period, a comparable task.

Enthusiasm was necessary, as Mr. L. W. M. had said. So too was the strict discipline imposed by the communist party and perhaps also its more drastic measures, the egalitarian mystique of collective ownership and the confidence given to the humblest by the disappearance of speculation and profit.

'There are other results, other forms of progress, other enterprises,' said Mr. L. W. M., 'which I would agree to place in another category. These have a less direct relation with the communist revolution and one could more easily imagine that they could have been carried out without the régime. But could it have been so if the soil had not already been deeply ploughed? I doubt it very much. And can one say to the revolution: now that the clearing up has been done, get out?

'In any event, it is natural that one gives credit to a régime for its intentions and accomplishments, even were one able to conceive of them without it.

'Firstly, there has been a progressive and general improvement in the standard of life of the masses, to the detriment, however, of those who had formerly the greater advantages and to the detriment also of a policy of quality.

'To sum up what I mean,' said Mr. L. W. M., 'I will make use of the following comparison. Previously, the rich ate rice and flour and the poor ate maize. Now everyone eats rice and flour but the quality of the rice and flour is not so good.

'Beside the material improvement, there has also been intellectual improvement. The two problems are intimately linked. I am not speaking here of what one calls cultural questions of art and literature. I am speaking of the "vital minimum" of the spirit, of the problem of the illiterates. How can economic progress be conceivable, how can even your capitalism be conceivable, not to speak of democratic liberties, amid a host of analphabetics? Do not forget, never forget, that in 1949 there were ninety per cent of illiterates in China.'

'As in Pakistan,' I said.

'Without doubt, and the comparison of the progress made would be interesting as a comparison of the régimes.

'There, too, you can realise all the differences from the situation in Russia. I am not speaking of the Soviet Union of to-day, but rather of the Russia of 1917. Certainly there were many illiterates at that time; generally speaking, it was estimated that fifty per cent of the Russians could read and write; in China only ten per cent.

'Much can be done in a country where one person in two could, technically and as a citizen, be made use of: but one in ten!

'Without doubt the régime has not solved this problem, but it has begun to tackle it. We have definitely been able to salvage twenty million illiterates. That is an honourable result, even though relatively small. However, there are still seventy million illiterates undergoing instruction. By the end of next year the percentage will have diminished to less than eighty per cent.'

I have seen everywhere, I must confess, this vast humming evening class that is China. In the factories, classes for workers; in the dormitories of the people's tenements, on every storey, deducted from the indispensable minimum, there are school-rooms. In the schools themselves, freed of the pupils in the evenings, in the pagodas too, there are for two hours twice a week classes for housewives; some quite young and often pregnant, others, the older ones, poring over their primers in their spectacles, reminding one of an illustration, infinitely multiplied, for 'The Mother' by Gorki. Everywhere there are voluntary teachers, unpaid and often moreover of modest attainments. Even as in this country one often sees children of eight or ten, carrying on their backs brats of two or three years old, so also one often sees semi-illiterates handing on to the analphabetics their minimum dose of five hundred characters a year.[1]

[1] This is a suitable point to raise the essential problem of the Chinese script. A Special Commission has decided for the adoption of the Latin alphabet, but the final decision has not yet been made. It is a difficult question, which divides the Chinese and the French as well; we spent an evening discussing it at the little Restaurant of the Three Tables with M. Etiemble and his colleagues, themselves divided into camps. M. Etiemble would open a controversy with Mme. Simone de Beauvoir even as, it seems, the Chinese Minister of Culture with the Chinese Minister of Education. I do not feel myself in any way qualified to act as arbitrator. But, in common sense, it seems to me sure that the Chinese language and writing, not only because of their difficulty but also by the impossibility of transscription and lack of phonetization, are largely responsible for the extraordinary decadence of Chinese civilization in modern times. (A similar observation is valid, to a lesser degree, for Arabic. The success of the Turkish reform is evident, and in Tunis M. Bourguiba has a plan for the vowels.) Is it possible to 'unhook' the writing from the language, which has imposed on it this remarkable inconvenience? That is the technical problem on which I hesitate to commit myself. Were it only possible, it would be highly desirable. The two great opportunities of the Chinese régime in the near future could well be the redemption of the virgin lands and the reform of the alphabet.

Repression

'Yes, great results have been achieved. But at what price?'

There has been talk of eight million victims.

'No figure is official. The size of the exaggeration is exactly one zero. I think that eight hundred thousand would be more probable though even that, in my opinion, would be excessive.

'The figures quoted are of foreign origin and contestable. Do not think, however, that our authorities are always trying to minimize the importance of the repression. They might even have a contrary tendency, in order to discourage any impulse towards rebellion![1] However that may be, we do not deny either the repression or even its excesses. Mao Tse-Tung and Chou En-Lai have, in any case, admitted them.'

'Yes, but have they done nothing to redress them?'

Mr. L. W. M. went on without hearing me.

'Has it not been so in every revolution? The French Revolution, for instance, and even nearer to you in your own Liberation? Apply the population coefficient and you can reckon your own figures. None the less, the Liberation did not raise the same questions. There had been no civil war.'

'Over and above the repression that followed the time of troubles, was there not a recurrence several years later, in 1953?'

'Yes, at the time of the campaign against the five classes of counter-revolutionaries. There were fresh executions in 1953; then their number lessened and from 1955 onwards there have been none at all.

'Do not forget, furthermore, that we are still in a state of war with Formosa.'

'But is there not still police supervision? Arrests, imprisonments?'

'Yes, this form of repression still exists, but it is rarely

[1] It is to be noted that in his latest speech Mr. Chou En-Lai does not give figures, but only percentages.

arbitrary. There is always, somewhere, a fact even if it has been exaggerated or badly interpreted.'

'Haven't you yourself, among your personal friends, someone who is to-day in prison and does not deserve to be?'

'One of my friends was arrested on the charge of harbouring a counter-revolutionary. He is still in prison. None the less, he has been given a Medal of Socialist Merit for having organized a drama school in the prison.'

Such anecdotes seem to me to be significant. The Chinese state is by no means meek and mild, but it is economical to the point of miserliness of the human material at its disposal. It does not want to lose anyone who might serve it, even were it in the most menial manner.

It may well be that such a system of repression, with its unforeseen changes and its penetentiary fantasies attains a more realistic and rigorous control than the demonstrations of police force in other countries which are very much more evident and more offensive to our feelings.[1]

The Opposition

It is always a difficult matter to find and get in touch with the opposition in a totalitarian country. The Chinese character, formed by centuries of Confucianism, is not the most transparent.

Smooth and polished like the stage masks at the Pekin Opera, the 'face' reflects the exterior and not the interior; it neither conveys nor betrays the vagaries of the soul.

It is not the present régime, despite its merits and even though it can provoke enthusiasm, that will tear off these masks and permit sincerity to break through. The prudent behaviour that it inspires

[1] Another example, in a very different field. A young Chinese girl student fell in love with a foreign colleague; her relations, her neighbours, the street superintendent covered her with reproaches about the liaison of which they did not approve. She resisted and her friend, losing patience, complained to his Ambassador; how can love be contrary to socialist doctrine? The Ambassador passed on his complaints to the Chinese authorities. Result: officials came to find the young girl and expressed their regrets and excuses. Another result: three weeks later, she was transferred to another university a thousand kilometres away.

in all well advised persons reinforces the atavistic fascination of imperturbability.

A western friend still living in China frequently received the free confidences of certain Chinese friends over whom he had some influence. One day one of them said, after talking quite openly to him: 'You understand; these are things that I do not say even to my wife.'

Thus the traveller in China has very little chance to meet a real member of the opposition, or at least to hear him define himself as such. Without doubt one could put forward as an objection the somewhat official nature of my own stay; but I notice, after reading several different accounts, that even the most free and daring of reporters has, for the most part, had no better luck.

'Rather than speak of an opposition', said Mr. L. W. M., 'it would be more exact to speak of various classes of persons in opposition.

'I will only mention for purposes of record the foreign agents, spies and saboteurs. They exist, though their number is sometimes exaggerated for tactical reasons and their number and importance are, in any case, difficult to estimate. This category does not enter into the classes of which we are speaking, for it does not really belong to the population of China. It is a foreign group.

'There are, on the other hand, all those people who have been placed at a disadvantage by the régime, from the large landlords to the most carefully handled capitalists. Certain of these have rallied to the régime, others are resigned to it, but there are some who have not forgiven it and who are "against" — without drawing from this any reasonable or even logical conclusions.

'There are some who criticize the political organization and would like it to be more liberal.

'There are some who criticize the economic system, either as a whole or in some one or other of its aspects. Their criticism is not generally, or even very frequently, a capitalist criticism. Many have been seduced by what they have heard tell of the system in Yugoslavia, would like to know more about it and are already inclined to move in that direction. The trip of Marshal Tito to China is heralded as a great success; it will be a great event.

'These various forms of criticism may also be combined. They are lucid and intelligent.

'Then there are those in opposition who rebel against a specific measure and who may therefore, according to their temperament, conceive a general hostility to the régime. Thus the law on marriage provoked lively opposition. It permits young persons to get married at eighteen and twenty years respectively without the consent of their parents which, hitherto, had been necessary at any age; it has resulted in an excess of births.

'Naturally there are the malcontents, the disaffected. These often express their dissatisfaction against the communists. I wish to make myself clear; not always against the régime, but against the Party members whom they reproach for their arrogance, their remoteness from the people; they are the mandarins of to-day. From this, there arises a sort of anti-communism, as elsewhere there is an anti-parliamentarism or an anti-semitism. This was the reason for the present '*cheng feng*' campaign which aims at re-educating party members. But many of these malcontents are not really in opposition. Their slogan might well be: "With Mao against the Party." '

I tried to get, at least approximately, a proportional evaluation of the opposition.

'It is very difficult to say, for the reasons that I have told you. How to find the line of demarcation between personal, specific or temporary dissatisfaction and a real opposition tendency. . . .'

'It has been said that, in certain regions, the opposition is as much as seventy per cent.'

'That does not seem to me possible. Thirty per cent would seem to me a maximum and that only in the most impressionable areas. . . .'

Whatever may be the truth about the opposition in China, it must be admitted that its potential is limited on the one hand by the effect of the policy of reconstruction and unity, while on the other, the great discredit that the last pre-communist régime has left in the public memory must never be forgotten.

To conclude on a more picturesque note, I would like to record that part of our conversation which dealt with this last subject, even though, perhaps, it may be a little in contradiction with the rest. But Mr. L. W. M., like a good Chinese, is not always strictly logical.

'But there are, none the less, supporters of the former régime?'

'Yes, there are. I have friends who say: "what China needs is an Emperor." '

'And supporters of the Kuo Min Tang? Or of Chiang Kai-Shek?'

Mr. L. W. M. sighed and passed to the offensive.

'Now it is my turn', he said, 'to ask you some questions. You know that we have suppressed begging in China. None the less, have you seen any beggars?'

'Yes, I have seen precisely two.'

'Have you met any thieves?'

'I have had no personal experiences of this sort, but I saw an illustrated poster at the door of a Canton restaurant warning against bicycle thieves.'

'True, but that is specifically applicable to Canton. In that city, which has easy communications with abroad, there are a certain number of foreign bicycles which have not received their registration plates and their removal is therefore somewhat easier. Let us go on. Have you seen any drunkards?'

'I have not seen any, but I have been told that they exist, though in small numbers; that they drink sorghum alcohol for preference and that they get drunk when fasting but never after a meal.'

'Have you seen any dogs?'

'I know that they have been condemned for reasons of

public hygiene and that they are only permitted in the countryside where they can render certain services. I have seen one near Pekin, in the first village to the south, guarding a backyard. His master, a Moslem, is a lover of animals. He asked me about dogs in France. And I saw another, one day, gaily crossing the street in Pekin. I do not know what for. . . .'

'You have heard of the great campaign to exterminate flies? None the less, have you seen any flies?'

'I saw two at Sian and even managed to kill one of them, thus making my contribution to the building of socialism. . . .'

'Excellent,' said Mr. L. W. M. 'I congratulate you. Many visitors know more than you and yet have not seen so much. Very well, your experience shows that one can still find beggars and thieves in China, though they have been proscribed and are only in small numbers; that one can still find flies, even though they have been exterminated, and dogs even though they have been forbidden. But what you will not find in the whole of China is anyone who has a nostalgia for the Nankin Government, an authentic supporter of the Kuo Min Tang, or a sincere admirer of Chiang Kai-Shek. . . .'

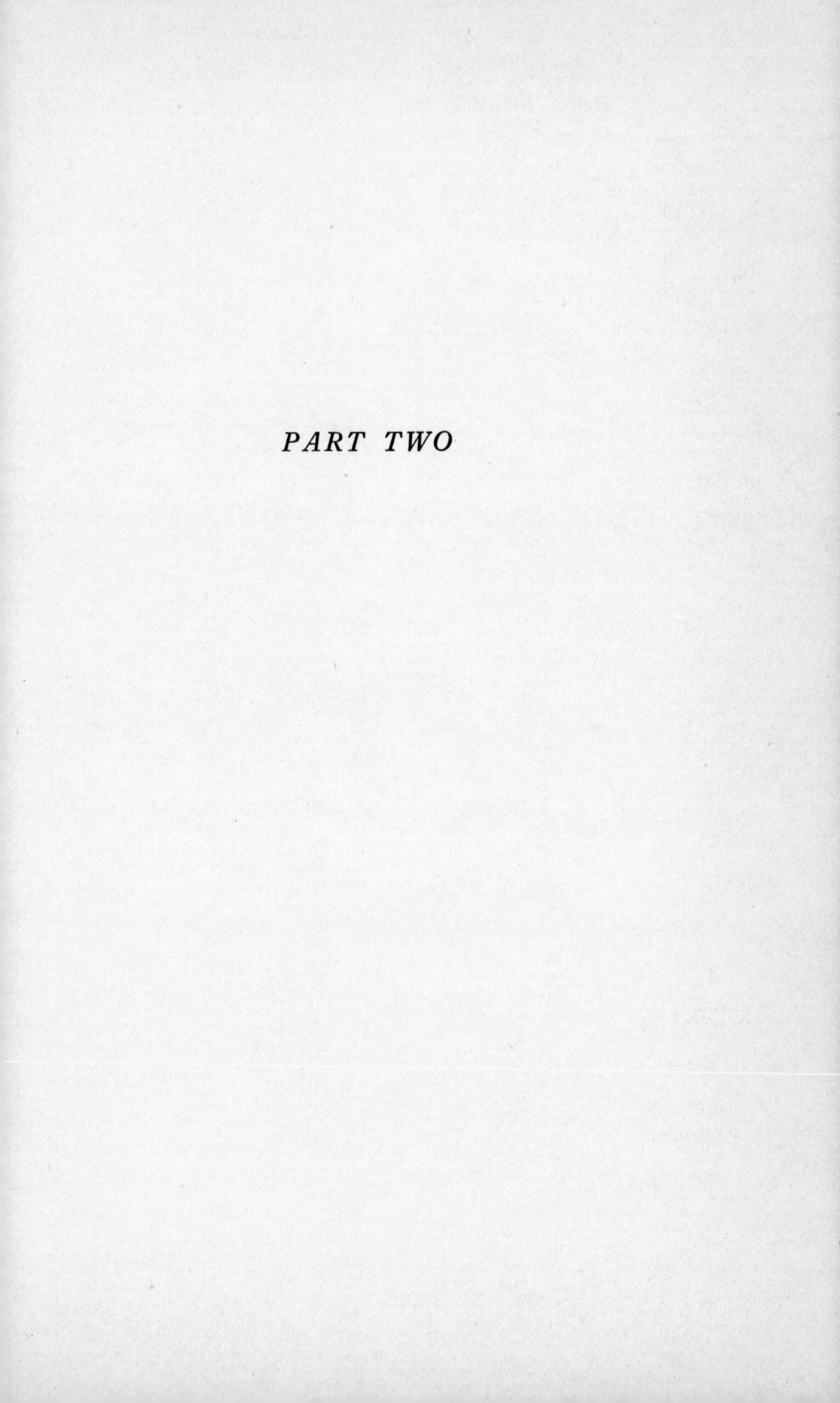

PART TWO

CHAPTER VI

COMMUNISM IN THE CHINESE WAY

IF I HAVE insisted on reporting my conversation with Mr. L. W. M., it is because it seemed to me to make a good introduction to the study which I now propose to make of the originality of the communist system in China.

'Communism in China cannot be pure communism. There must be something different in it. The Chinese never do anything quite like the rest of the world. . . .'

How many times have I heard this said, especially in Europe!

In China itself, one of the persons with whom I talked told me: 'China has been Buddhist for a very long time, and yet she has never been really Buddhist. We have made Buddhism Chinese, we made the Manchu Emperors Chinese and we can make communism Chinese.'

I remarked, with a certain amount of pedantry, that if Buddhism had changed its form in China, it was perhaps partly due to the fact that it had been not a little persecuted.[1] This is certainly not the case with Marxism; and as far as the Manchu Emperors are concerned, one could hardly regard them as doctrinaires.

Is there such a thing as Chinese communism?

What is it?

One must, indeed, be distrustful of the phrase 'Chinese communism', above all in a country where, in the past, so much effort and formal logic were called upon to demonstrate the famous thesis: 'White horse is not horse.'

If one understands by 'Chinese communism' a system which

[1] Simone de Beauvoir: 'Persecuted Buddhism only survived by degrading itself, etc. . . .' *The Long March*, pp. 228 *et. seq.*

would be other than communism, or which would be *less* than communism, or in which the *present evolution* would depart in any way from communist doctrine; even more definitely, if it is believed that it is already engaged in 'the third way' between capitalism and socialism, or even that this third way is taking form from now on towards the future, then I may say at once for the better understanding of this study, that this is a mistake.

But one can speak without fear of equivocation of 'communism in the Chinese way'. Because the advent of the communist régime in China was accompanied, as we have seen, by special conditions; because, while taking account of these conditions — and, moreover, provoking them to some extent — and acting according to the logic of their thought and the urges of their character, the Chinese leaders have made use of methods which are all their own; because the conjunction of these conditions and these methods has given birth to specific institutions which give to communism in China an original aspect and, without any doctrinal renunciation, distinguish it sharply from the Soviet model.

The conditions which accompanied the advent of communism, and those resulting from the nine years of its progressive and fruitful management of great national affairs, explain how it was able to obtain from the start and was able to keep, to enlarge and to consolidate the co-operation and support of all classes of the population; that is to say, not only in those classes which normally would seem the most receptive, the wage-earners and the poor peasants, not only among those who are politically or economically indifferent, but even among those classes and sectors normally and logically antagonistic.

Certainly, it was by undertaking a great national task, in getting China out of the rut, that the régime was able to multiply the number of communists and, over and above this, to attract to its support the non-communists also. But, in order to carry out this task fully, the régime had need of the most extensive co-operation, even including therein the so-called 'refractory sectors'.

That is what the genius of Mao Tse-Tung has understood, even as it understood the necessity of hastening agrarian reform and of stirring up a revolution of the peasants and not only of the workers, of the peasants *even more than the workers*.

'Without the United Front, in the largest possible conception, unifying the overwhelming majority of the population, the victory of the Revolution would have been impossible', Mao told me.

We have gone far beyond the idea of Her Majesty's Opposition!

We have reached that of an 'auxiliary opposition'. The most typical and the most important instance is that of the bourgeoisie (including the intellectuals). Auxiliary bourgeois cadres have been created in a workers' and peasants' state. There are also the religious cults in an atheist state. A similar idea, combined with other considerations, is to be found in the policy followed towards the national minorities. Also in the policy concerning the Chinese overseas, which is not only to be explained by a preoccupation at seeing foreign currencies return to the country; there are eleven million overseas Chinese, mostly bourgeois in origin and not communist in opinion. The régime has no intention of neglecting this supporting force in internal affairs and propaganda force in external affairs. With the greatest care and circumspection it seeks to associate it, though outside the country, with the régime.

Exception and counter-indication: the class of large landowners and rich peasants. No effort has been made to attach them to the régime. For them there has been no compensation, not the slightest care or consideration. They are regarded as technically useless and ideologically irreconcilable.

The essential idea of communism in the Chinese way, the origin of its divergent peculiarities is to be found then in these words: the United Front — and in the United Front it is the question of the bourgeoisie that is all-important.

CHAPTER VII

THE CONTRACT WITH THE MIDDLE CLASSES—THE UNITED FRONT

IN MY introduction I spoke of the conquest and assimilation of the middle classes. I also spoke of 'dressage'. These expressions are correct. None the less, I would prefer to use here, for the developments which are to follow, the *idea of a contract with the middle classes*. For this idea of a contract is better adapted to an explanation of the United Front.

The middle classes are not normally in their place in a workers' and peasants' state. They can only take their place in such a state by first playing with words and speaking of the 'working people', a conception which might be enlarged to include the lower middle classes and the intellectuals, as Mao Tse-Tung has frequently said, but could only be extended with great difficulty to the upper middle classes referred to as 'national'.

This is, none the less, what has been done. Both words and men have been turned to their use. A real contract has resulted. The communist state has decided to approach the middle classes, but has made, none the less, certain discriminations:

1. First of all there are the lower middle classes, near to the other classes by their methods of making a living.
2. Secondly there is the so-called 'national' section which is part of the upper middle class and is so called because, on the one hand it represented Chinese interests alone, to the exclusion of foreign capitalism, and on the other since it has given proof of its willingness to support 'the liberation'.
3. There remain finally the bureaucratic capitalists, that is to say those elements of the business classes which had

close connections with foreign finance or which had refused to give any proof of national spirit, these two characteristics being supposed to go hand in hand for the convenience of the thesis.

This last category has been cast into outer darkness, like the rural landowners.

It was in this way that the United Front was formed.

The United Front officially comprises four classes; workers, peasants, lower middle classes and the 'national' classes.

Some people think that the four little stars which form an arc around the larger star in the national emblem represent these four classes. But this interpretation, I am bound to say, is not confirmed by Chinese officials, who simply say that there ought to be five stars, since everything in China goes by fives. . . .

So a contract was proposed to the lower middle classes and the 'national' classes. Why?

Because on the one hand, their *immediate* co-operation had appeared indispensable to success. They represented a far from negligible element of both action and opinion.

Because on the other hand, their *permanent* co-operation had appeared necessary to provide the new régime with indispensable technical cadres.

It is in this contract with the middle classes that the historical progress of the Chinese revolution differs essentially from that of the Soviet revolution.

It is easy to imagine how much the progress of the Soviet economy would have been made easier, how different life in Russia would have become, had the régime been able to preserve the co-operation of the best of its emigrés.

The middle classes, or rather the Chinese middle classes, have, on their side, accepted this contract.

Why?

Partly, without doubt, for idealism and for those patriotic considerations which we have already mentioned.

Partly, also, for more material reasons. Because they gained certain advantages thereby. And because they could not do otherwise. . . . The 'campaigns' have made that plain enough. . .'

This contract has assured the integration of the middle classes into the workers' and peasants' state, politically in the form of the United Front and economically under the forms known as the mixed economy.

But, and we cannot stress this too heavily, this integration, even though it constitutes the main originality of Chinese communism, does not involve any renunciation of communist doctrines. For it has intervened as a temporary measure. It is not a contract of *installation*, it is a contract of *adaptation*.

The middle classes have been integrated with the final aim of their disappearance as classes.

The capitalists, valued as cadres, must normally become wage earners of the upper category.

When Burnham wrote 'The Managerial Revolution', he laid stress on the distinction between managerial and capitalist functions and underlined the rise of the one at the expense of the other.

Certainly Mao Tse-Tung has made no managerial revolution, but it is not too much to say that he has taken pains to make the revolution *with* the managers, to retain the capitalist middle classes as administrative and managerial groups to provide irreplacable specialists.

Similar methods and a similar contract apply to the intellectuals, the 'mind managers' of literature, art, science and education. Here, however, because of the difference of the initial factors, we do not find any special institutions such as the mixed economy. There would only be, at the present time, the test of a general watchword, with the Hundred Flowers and the Hundred Schools.

A conception as remarkable as a contract between the communist state and the middle classes, an institution as original as the United Front, could not be built up from one day to the next and could not develop in perfect harmony. Moreover, since it was a matter of a contract of adaptation, the situation could not be static, and its evolution has not ceased to develop and is still developing at the present time. Some might consider it as an unbroken process of creation, others as a permanent struggle aiming at progressive and precautionary extermination. This evolution is not developing in a regular and tranquil rhythm. There have been alternate phases of crisis and relaxation. The crises are the campaigns; the campaigns of the past — the Wu-Fan or 'Five Antis', directed against the business classes (that is to say, officially, against the right-wing and refractory elements of the middle classes) the 're-moulding' campaign and the campaign against Hu Feng and Hu Fengism, directed against the bourgeois intellectuals (similar comment) and, finally, the present campaigns which are still confusedly being carried on and which have one interesting feature in that the initial campaign, '*cheng-feng*' or 'rectification', was aimed *at* the communist party in order to reform it, and not at its associates. It is, moreover, normal that the United Front should provoke crises within the Party itself and there have been instances of this in the past. But, as we shall see, this campaign has been transformed, rapidly enough, into a counter-campaign against the right-wing deviationists of the middle classes, of the intellectuals and of the non-communist political parties.

I intend to analyse the present campaigns, the twists and turns of whose evolution I have been able to follow during my brief stay in China, whilst giving, in order to make the subject intelligible, a brief resumé of previous crises.

But first of all it is necessary to devote an explanatory chapter to the political institutions of the United Front, that is to say to the small parties and the Consultative Conference.

CHAPTER VIII

THE POLITICAL PARTIES—THE CONSULTATIVE CONFERENCE

IT IS the policy of assimilation and, more especially, the contract with the middle classes which clearly explains the existence in China of non-communist political parties and, at the same time, the real nature of those parties.

In actual fact, it might be asked if it be exact to speak of non-communist parties. For these different parties have no divergence of doctrine or programme either with each other or with the Communist Party. They are, to some extent, communist parties with socially differentiated membership. In their conferences in 1949, they all declared officially, at the time of the first meeting of the Consultative Conference, that they accepted the leadership of the Chinese Communist Party and that they accepted as their own the general communist party programme.

What distinguishes these parties is, in fact, solely the social or professional origin of their members.

There are at the moment seven such parties, recruited from the middle classes and the intellectuals. The most important of them is the Democratic League, for the most part of middle class and intellectual membership (30,000 members).[1] The most specialized party is the Party of Democratic Construction which includes only capitalists, industrialists and merchants of a certain standing; for this reason the subscription is higher

[1] This party first appeared in 1941 as a merger between various already existing organizations. After a period of expectation, it took up a stand against the Kuo Min Tang in 1944, underwent a schism and various persecutions and was reformed in Hong Kong, whence its leaders returned to China after the communist victory.

than in the other parties, being from 7 to 10 yuan a month (25,000 members).[1] The Revolutionary Committee of the Kuo Min Tang is explained by historical reasons; it groups together the former adherents of Chiang Kai-Shek who have disavowed him and gone over to communism (16,000 members). The Party of Democratic Advancement comprises mainly teachers of the first and second grades. It is particularly developed in the Shanghai region. Then there are also:

A Democratic Peasants' and Workers' Party which, despite its name, has a lower middle class membership. This party, founded in 1928 and previously called the Tien Party, was the result of historical circumstances also.

An Association of September 24th (savants).

A Democratic League of Formosa.

Lastly there is a group of overseas Chinese whom one cannot really consider as forming a party.

It is difficult enough to disentangle this skein of little parties, some of which are only distinguishable by past events, and who often enough practise a double allegiance, to the benefit of the oldest amongst them, the Democratic League.

All these parties taken together represent about a hundred thousand members, as against twelve to fourteen million members of the Communist Party (the latter figure if its satellite organizations are taken into account).

'We are not parties in your sense of the word, which present themselves at elections with their own programmes', I was told. 'However that is all the better for us, for otherwise we should be crushed out of existence!'

'Is it possible to form new parties?'

'Undoubtedly it would be possible but naturally on one condition, that they accept socialism.'

'Have there been any cases of the sort?'

[1] For the other parties, the subscription is variable, either one yuan or less a month. In the communist party the subscription is progressive and proportionate to salary — 1 per cent up to 100 yuan, 2 per cent from 100 to 200 yuan, etc.

'Not as regards new parties, but the possibility of reviving an old party — the Union for the Salvation of the Country — is now being studied. Then there have been mergers and there may be more in the future.'

The activity of these parties is shown in various ways. They have certain papers to express their views (the *Clarity — Kuang Ming Jih Pao* — for their common views, the *Ta Kung Pao* for the industrialists and merchants, the *Shanghai Information Journal*, etc.).

Members of the different parties participate in the National Assembly and in the provincial assemblies. But they do not figure there as such and do not constitute groups.

Members of these parties are also prominent in the principal town councils, where they seem especially singled out to welcome and entertain western visitors. With a single exception, I have always been received by an 'assistant-mayor' belonging to one of the democratic parties. In the different capitals, I was similarly received by a Vice-President of the Consultative Conference, also chosen from among the non-communists. At the apex of the pyramid, a third of the ministers, sixteen as against thirty-two communist, are either non-party (as Mr. Chang Hsi-Jo) or members of the democratic parties (like the two women ministers and the three rebels already mentioned). We will return to this subject in connection with the present crisis.

Finally, the United Front is the spirit behind an original institution, the Consultative Conference, which exists at the national level and also in each of the six provinces. It must not be overlooked that, in these organizations, the Communist Party is not in the majority. A Conference of this sort includes representatives of the parties, of the communists, and of the womens' and youth organizations, as well as representatives of the religious cults, the national minorities, the overseas Chinese and a certain number of 'invited' members.

This institution was first conceived by Chiang Kai-Shek. It has been most ingeniously resurrected by the communist régime. It played a most important role in the early days before the creation of an elective assembly; and it still functions very regularly. In Pekin it is housed in a fine Parliament Building, with a great assembly hall, which is only used two or three times a year, when there are plenary sessions. Between sessions this hall is sometimes lent for theatrical presentations and it was in it, seated before a rostrum, that I saw the Pekin Opera for the first time.

The activities of the Conference are carried out primarily by a Permanent Committee chosen from its members, and whose meetings are more frequent (several times a month). When I entered the Palace of the Consultative Conference for the second time, to attend a meeting arranged there with the leaders of the Democratic Parties, I was told that the Permanent Committee had been in session for several days. To do what? I asked. To discuss the transformation of the province of Kuangsi into an autonomous region.

The exact role of the Conference is shown by its name — 'to confer' and 'to consult'.

'In this country', said my informants, 'we are always consulting. We are in no hurry and we must come to an agreement. There is never any division of opinion on problems, for, before solving them, we have all come to an unanimous decision. We go on consulting until we have reached it. . . .'

We know that the Chinese know how to wait. They also love 'to consult'.

The Conferences are consulted, I was told, on all sorts of subjects, even on the appointment of senior officials. It seems, in fact, that the 'scope' of the competence of these bodies is very broad. The question of the actual exercise of their competence, of the efficacy of their intervention, is evidently quite another matter.

It would, I think, be a mistake to consider the small parties as simply a façade, mainly intended for political visitors from the western democracies.

Among the non-communist leaders there are persons who are by no means negligible. Even without speaking of Mr. Chang Hsi-Jo, who is a non-party man, I have been able to size up a number of them by personal contact, though none of them, during these meetings, ever confided in me in any way or expressed other than the orthodox views. But, as we shall see, some of them have taken risks during the *cheng-feng* crisis. We shall see, too, that the Communist Party, despite the overwhelming disproportion of forces, is quick to take fright whenever the little parties raise their voices, even when they have been expressly summoned.

In the logic of the system, these parties can call on persons of technical value on condition that they are politically amenable. But they must not in any event constitute a force — not even a compensating force, not to speak of an opposition — but may only be a balancing factor. They are weights in the scale which need not be considered unless they are on the credit side. They must be a source of information and influence for the government and the Party executive. They are a gratification granted to the middle classes who must consider themselves flattered and fortunate not to have disappeared altogether from the political scene and the '*cursus honorum*'.

They also make it possible for certain groups among the intellectuals and business men to be kept under control. By the logic of the contract of transition, they are preparing certain middle-class elements, either immediately or in the next generation, for eventual selection and recruitment for the Communist Party.

An eminent professor and writer told me: 'I belong to the Democratic League, but I am preparing to enter the Communist Party one day. I am in no hurry to do so.'

At Sian, the Vice-President of the Consultative Conference, a former Professor of Yenan University in the time of troubles, a man who was very well informed on international, and even on French, politics, had a double allegiance; he was at the same time a member of the Democratic League and of the Communist Party.

Many times when talking with leading industrialists, members, as they were bound to be, of the Party of Democratic Construction, and deputies at various assemblies and conferences, I have heard said: 'My children do not want any inheritance. My son is a Communist Party member.'

Thus there is a double evolution, the other aspect of which we shall see in the course of our study of the economic structure of the country.

Note

Without any pretence of making an exhaustive study of the subject and simply to clarify our ideas, I give below certain details concerning the representation of the 'little parties'.

In the National Assembly (where, however, it is not a question of the representation of the parties as such, but simply a record of the number of deputies belonging to each category):

Democratic League	82
Revolutionary Committee of the Kuo Min Tang	59
Democratic Construction	63
Democratic Advancement	16
Democratic Peasants' and Workers' Party	19
Overseas Chinese	4
Association of September 24th	24
Democratic League of Formosa	2
Communist Youth Movements	5
Various	284
Communist Party	668
Total	1,226

In the National Consultative Conference:

Communist Party	40 only
Kuo Min Tang	25

Democratic League	25
Democratic Construction	25
Peasants' and Workers' Party	12
Democratic Advancement	12
Overseas Chinese	6
Association of September 24th	12
Democratic League of Formosa	6
Young Communists	10
'Invited members'	255

CHAPTER IX

THE CRISES OF THE UNITED FRONT—IDEOLOGICAL RE-MOULDING—THE FIVE ANTIS

ALTHOUGH I make no pretence here of writing a historical study, I feel that it is not possible fully to understand the phenomenon of the United Front without knowing at least the broad outlines of the main crises through which it passed between 1950 and 1952.

One of these, the ideological 're-moulding', particularly concerned the intellectuals. The other, the 'Five Antis', specially affected the industrial and commercial classes (including therein the lower middle classes and even the smallest of the merchants and shopkeepers).

I. IDEOLOGICAL RE-MOULDING AND THE HU FENG AFFAIR[1]

Mao Tse-Tung has always paid close attention to the problem of the 'intellectuals'. They must be retained, but must be freed from bourgeois ideology. They must be 'helped to overcome their prejudices and be won over to the Front in the service of the workers'.

For that reason, 'their ideology must once again be placed in the mould'.

Mao has given a living example of this aim, in one of his speeches at Yenan, in which he recalled his own experience.

[1] As a rule the expression ideological 'reform' has been used, but the translation is a poor one, and I prefer to use the word 're-moulding', for reasons which will shortly become clear.

Mao remembered that he had himself been an intellectual and had fostered bourgeois prejudices. 'When I was a student,' he said, 'I considered it beneath my dignity to carry out the lightest manual labour, even to carry my own luggage. I would willingly enough have worn the garments of another student, but I would never have put on the clothes of a peasant or a worker, for I would have thought them dirty.' Later, Mao served in the revolutionary armies with workers, peasants and simple soldiers. He got to know them, and they got to know him. Now, it was the intellectuals 'who have not yet been re-moulded' who seemed to him dirty, and he knew that 'the workers and the peasants are the cleanest people in the world, even if their hands are filthy and their feet covered in cow-dung. . . .

'That is what it means to replace the feelings of one class with those of another. . . . If our artists and writers want their works to be welcomed by the masses, they must transform and re-mould their thoughts and their feelings. Without such a transformation, without such a re-moulding, they can do nothing that is good and they will be unsuited for any kind of work.'

Re-moulding is, then, a thing of lasting value; despite the example chosen it is not applicable to intellectuals alone. Every bourgeois may be called upon to re-mould his ideology, as every communist to 'rectify his way of life'. But over and above this lasting value, this expression designated a campaign which developed between the summer of 1950 and the summer of 1952 and which concerned 'various types of intellectuals'.[1] It was a question of creating the new man, of 'casting out the old herds', a Chinese equivalent of our phrase 'casting out the old man'.

I was struck by the similarity of phrasing with that of conversion in the Catholic church, especially in the experience of Pascal; the 'old man' and the 'new heart'.

The official propaganda documents of the time painstakingly

[1] Mao, October 23rd, 1951.

enumerate and even classify the vicious spiritual traits which must be cast out — in fact the twelve mortal sins.[1]

Nobody will be surprised to learn that the methods advocated were criticism and self-criticism and the exercises recommended were the assiduous study of marxism-leninism and 'mao-tse-tungism', or that the committees and sub-committees of reform divided their labours according to regions and professions.

Mr. Chien Chun-Juei, who was at the time Assistant Minister of Culture, played a leading role in the development of this campaign, drawing on the lessons of his experience in the Pekin-Tientsin area and extending them to the whole country, stigmatizing the admiration too often accorded to American institutions, wealth and technique and exalting the creative power of the Chinese people. In the higher educational institutions, committees of economic control doubled their offensive for ideological re-education and it was discovered as an undoubted fact that those who were bad ideologists were to be found among those who were bad administrators. Offensives followed conferences and denunciations followed reports. Thousands of participants sent in written accounts of the improvements they had made in themselves and of the

[1] 1. Feudal mentality (including the arrogance of the man of letters and his repugnance towards manual labour).
2. Egoism (consideration of special interest to the detriment of the general good).
3. The idea of 'face'.
4. Familiarism (putting the group above the nation: excess of family feeling and the widespread network of relationships was the reason for countless abuses in the old China).
5. Individualism (as opposed to team spirit and to the taste for group meetings and 'conferences').
6. Individual heroism (lust for personal glory — swank).
7. Hedonism.
8. Red tape.
9. Opportunism.
10. Idealism (in contrast to Marxist materialism).
11. Corruption.
12. The 'middleman' mentality (which was particularly widespread in the great ports and which took the form of a mixture of mercantile ambition and servile behaviour towards foreigners).

zeal which they had shown with regard to others. The river of reform rolled confessions along like pebbles. The most garrulous submission did not guarantee impunity, but the rigours of repression were limited to a general mortification of spirits and to the dismissal of a few professors.

The re-moulding campaign slackened after this paroxysm, the universities fell back once more into their daily routine, and the intellectuals were to know two full years of respite until the Hu Feng affair (early 1955), which provoked the unleashing of a fresh campaign (judged less considerable, since Chou En-Lai did not mention it, but which, at the time, was given very great publicity). The facts are well known today and have been analysed in similar manner by observers of varied views. I will only refer to it, therefore, to note one feature which is of importance, since one finds it again most particularly in the present *cheng-feng* crisis. The condemnation of Hu Feng took several months and his famous declaration of the five daggers[1] was at first favoured by a wide official distribution. The régime seemed incapable of stopping in its first onrush a movement that was directed against it — or at least which it so regarded. Only let the courser do its tricks and gather speed before throwing the lasso. One could feel in the slowness of the defence reflex an element of surprise and embarrassment. The régime was put out of countenance before the behaviour of men who began to feel themselves becoming freer. Everything took place as if, after such long restraints, no one in the régime was able at first sight to recognize the signs of reawakened audacity. They rubbed their eyes and waited. They did not know whether to be excited or angry. They could not understand the reaction of the orthodox cadres (and the vigour of these reactions might too have been a cause for surprise — they took

[1] Again the fateful number — five. The memorandum sent by Hu Feng to the Central Committee of the Communist Party enumerated the five daggers planted in the brain of the Chinese writers, namely the necessity for adopting a Marxist viewpoint, the fusion of the writers with the workers and peasants, the recasting of thought, the use of a national style, and the use of literature for political aims.

offence at so little — did they think themselves threatened?).

It is less easy for subjects to forget how to act in free conditions than for rulers to forget how to reason in terms of freedom.

At the apogee of the *cheng-feng*, at the very moment when the graph was about to take a downward turn, a rumour spread, from a reliable though not official source, that Hu Feng was about to be set free. The event seemed at that time logical, yet at the same time a great sign of evolution. I took it into my head to ask if I might be permitted to meet him. My guide told me a little later that the rumour had not been confirmed. None the less, a doubt remained.

II. The Three Antis and the Five Antis (*San-Fan and Wu-Fan*)

The campaign known as the Five Antis has been the most serious trial to which the business classes have been subjected. It was dependent from the start on a different campaign on a lesser scale — and, if one may put it, aimed in a different direction — 'The Campaign of the Three Antis'. These were the three vices of officials and communists, which led to the five vices of the reactionaries and the bourgeois.

Unleashed at the end of 1951, the San-Fan movement, the Three Antis, was directed against corruption, wastage and bureaucratism. The administration was then being carried out partly by the former personnel inherited from the Kuo Min Tang, and it might have been feared that the detestable habits which had led that régime to disaster might still be flourishing; and partly by fresh teams lacking experience, who might commit errors or show themselves susceptible to temptation. On the advice of specialists, this movement was intended less to repress existing abuses and exactions — whose number should not be exaggerated — than to create a salutary terror and to favour an administrative changing of the guard. Spectacular penalties were imposed, principally on unjust judges. The sensational highlight was in February 1952, with the trial of seven leaders, before an audience installed in the concert hall of the Sun Yat-Sen park, with huge crowds and broadcasts of the hearings in public places, big shops, offices and schools. There were two death sentences. The trial established a legal precedent. There were to be other capital and also prison sentences, numerous degradations and dismissals. It was not only abuse of authority which was punished, but also instances of negligence, nepotism, favouritism and frivolity.

But it was very quickly realized that no one would have been corrupted had there been no one to corrupt them, that the administrative sores were due to the contagion of mercantile vices, and so, from the beginning of the first quarter of 1952, with the well-known taste for classification and the superstition attaching to the number five, the Wu-Fan movement began to take form, against the five vices attributed to 'merchant-traitors'. These are:

Bribery.
Fraud and tax evasion.
Theft of state property.
Sabotage of work and use of inferior materials (in public contracts).
Fraudulent procuring of state economic secrets.

The campaign assumed a particular virulence because of the continuance of the Korean War. Certain merchants were accused of furnishing the men at the front with faked medicaments, damaged foodstuffs and defective spare parts for lorries; criminal mercantilism or imperialist complicity? 'Let us strike at the tigers', big, medium or small tigers according to the amount of their profits.

Generally speaking, the pitch was higher than in the campaign for ideological re-moulding. Fevered criticism was replaced by wholesale denunciation. Students and secondary school boys were given a month's holiday to go through the informers' post-bags, verify commercial accounts and interrogate employees who, in bewilderment, sometimes asked their patrons to 'whisper' the misdeeds which might be brought home to them. This campaign did not only concern, as one might think, a small minority of business men belonging to the most well-to-do category but a very large proportion of the commercial classes including shopkeepers and second-hand dealers of the most wretched kind. It might even have been asked at one time whether it was not aimed at the commercial classes as a whole, as had been the case with the rural landowners. At Shanghai, out of 163,400 enterprises, 5 per cent only were convicted of gross violations, but 15 per cent only escaped unscathed. 50 per cent of the enterprises were classed as guilty of minor errors but treated with indulgence, while 30 per cent were considered 'semi-respectful of the law'.

At the moment, the campaign has already died down to some extent. It will come to an end whenever it may seem to result in the disorganization of certain economic sectors. If stopped in time, it will bring two definite advantages to the régime. A price reduction of 5 per cent, made possible by the selling-off of stocks and the discouragement of speculation; and a general reduction of fees to owners and directors, who are happy enough to have got off so cheaply. This experience is not unallied to the meekness with which the managers have since accepted the transitory régime of the mixed economy. It was at this time also that all the traders and industrialists were grouped together in the Industrial and Commercial Confederation.

CHAPTER X

CHENG-FENG—THE RECTIFICATION CAMPAIGN

THE *cheng-feng* and what I shall call the 'cluster of 1957 campaigns' (the rectification campaign, the campaign against the right-wing deviationists and the Hundred Flowers) are a most extraordinary group. One must be Chinese and, without doubt, also a good communist to understand them. At least, one must have been in China, as I was able to be, during the decisive weeks of May and June to understand that one does not understand....

When I arrived in China the campaign was in full swing. *Cheng-feng* was the sole subject of conversation. The hubbub about it had not yet reached western ears. However, I had brought with me the number of *Pravda* quoting the article in the *Jen Min Jih Pao* of April 14th, which explained its essential spirit while avoiding the letter (for the affair was only launched on May 1st) and under another name (for it was still a question of 'internal contradictions'). At Hong Kong, I had found in the local press an English editorial on the rectification campaign (I had not then grasped its relation to my Russian text about contradictions) and a paragraph on the anger of the Dean of the Peita University, Ma Yin-Chu, who found that the students had become insupportable with their new fad of 'criticism', and that nothing would be better than to suppress the Political Committees in the Universities, as there had been question of doing. (It is well known that all over the world students are irreverent critics and in China the great majority of them stem from the bourgeois classes).

Despite modern news processes, news from China wends its

way westward with the speed of the ocean liner (save when it is a question of some sensational item, which cannot be confirmed and which is generally ill-intentioned). Announced in Moscow on April 14th and in Pekin on May 1st, news of the *cheng-feng* arrived in Paris about the same time as I did, roughly on June 20th. The friends who met me and asked me about my trip could hardly wait for my replies before protesting against Mao's new speech which had just been published. But that speech was dated four months back and I had been aware of its essential features for ten weeks. In the meantime he had rewritten and reconsidered much of it, and in so far as anything of it still remained it was to be contradicted within forty-eight hours by Chou En-Lai in a speech before the National Assembly which was made public on the day it was delivered; it was not a regular session of the Assembly, for it had been re-convened for this event and the 1,226 deputies had hastened to Pekin from all the provinces of the vast land of China to take part in the great public session (to which I also was most fortunate to be invited), where they had to wait for eight hours while Mao's ink faded and Chou En-Lai's pen was sharpened, in order to rehearse fresh roles and prepare fresh masks.

Now that the *cheng-feng* campaign seems to have come to an end and has given way to an inverse campaign directed against the right-wing deviationists, we are getting delayed reports of the first and some not dissimilar echoes of the second at the same time. We read, in fragments, sensational declarations directed against the Communist Party and, which is even more sensational, that they have been taken from the columns of the official *Jen Min Jih Pao*; at the same time we learn that accusations had been made against the non-communist leaders, including members of the government, and that they had all, with a single exception, made expiatory confessions. We had been led to suppose some logical relation between the punishment and the malefactor, between the fiery denunciation and the penitent deviationist. Nothing of the kind! These denunciations which seemed to us so weighty, but at the same time so empty (for they were without details or any constructive suggestions) and, if I may say so, so stupid that one sometimes could not help thinking of a farce or a provocation, came for the most part from persons of no account; they were delivered in circumstances of minor importance and we do not know if their authors have got into trouble since the spotlight of publicity has not followed them beyond their first outburst. There was, for example, the University Professor who said, strangely enough in the circumstances, that one should kill communists; but he himself has killed no one and, up to the present, there is nothing to show that he in his turn has been threatened with death or even prison.[1] On the other hand, if we examine the case of the rebel leaders and ministers, we will, if we go back to the original sources, find their views moderate and even innocuous. Yet these, and these alone, have been adjudged dangerous. The very situation of these ministers is exceedingly strange; unmasked as enemies, they have not yet resigned as members of the government. Two of them have confessed and expressed contrition, the third has admitted nothing and continues to grumble. We shall only know later which of these tactics will have been the better inspired.

All this appears, however, relatively simple to those for whom the key of anti-communism opens even the most

[1] He was Professor Ko Pei-Chi. As criticism of sources is necessary for studying the history of past centuries, it is equally indispensable for contemporary events when dealing with the communist world and more particularly with China. We know nothing of the Professor's proposals either from his writings or even from a direct report but only, as we also find in other cases, from criticisms made against him. 'Comments were made', the *Jen Min Jih Pao* says on June 8th, 'on the erroneous opinions of Professor Ko Pei-Chi. Here is his last speech, etc....'

His statements appeared sensational when printed in the western press. Yet he does not seem to have said that communists must be killed, which even Senator McCarthy has never suggested, but only that they should be eliminated and even killed if they persisted in their errors. Here is the only precise example cited by this fiery Professor; last year, in order to improve the conditions of the intellectuals, the University decided to provide each of them with a personal servant; but this privilege was withdrawn on grounds of economy. These great declarations are, therefore, reduced to the question of a chambermaid. 'In our opinion,' writes a reader, 'this Professor Ko Pei-Chi must come out of his study.' In China too 'what is exaggerated is of no importance'.

oriental locks. When, after the events in Hungary, Mao appeared to be inspired by some semi-liberal views, it was regarded as a sign of weakness; the régime was cracking on all sides. But when the liberal trend was abandoned and there was a return to rigour, this was considered a fresh sign of weakness and of fear. Reasoning of this sort has gone on for a long time about the Chinese régime, as about the Soviet régime. Every sign of crisis, every symptom disconcerting for us, has been interpreted as an indication of the death-agony. It is because we do not want to make the effort of inquiring into the special laws that govern the lives of these régimes which no more than any others, cannot remain immobile. I would like in my turn to offer some preliminary keys which will open at least the outer gates of the enclosure.

The first of these keys is that the *cheng-feng* campaign, in the opinion of all serious observers, was not due to any external source or any preliminary pressure. Doubtless, there is serious discontent in China, but this discontent did not constitute, nor does it now constitute, a menace. The communist leaders have not yielded to any emergency, nor have they had to compromise with any demands. Their initiative was completely free and spontaneous.

Secondly, the Chinese character, which has been usually described as cold and secretive, is liable, probably more than many others, to exaltation, excess and exaggeration. These characteristics appear even more forcibly during the great campaigns. We must beware of the temptation of taking violent statements as basic facts when they are unfavourable to the régime, while rejecting them as without value when they are made on the other side. Even a cursory study of the political campaigns in China will easily furnish an anthology of the most ridiculous exaggerations. When at the launching of the San-Fan campaign (that of the Three Antis) the Mayor of Tsientsin announced: 'We call the Kuo Min Tang corrupt but we are ten times worse than they were,' this was not much more serious than the apologia of the good

University Professor for the massacre of the communists. There is less useful information in such a stupefying proposal, a good subject for a journalist's 'flash', than in some very subtle remark let fall by one of the leaders, or a word by word investigation of the prosy editorials of the *Jen Min Jih Pao*. There is a phenomenon which might be called 'psychological progression' which exists at the level of persons of a certain importance, such as those we have mentioned, but which can become almost mental derangement in backward regions and among the most backward masses (a remarkable example of this is given by the story of the swords and the magic gourds which we shall relate in Chapter XI). The verbal excess and the intoxication of mind that it reveals naturally follows the trend of the graph of the campaign, dying down when this begins to descend and following it upwards whenever it is given the impulse.

But if these psychological states are an effect of the rhythm of the great campaigns, they are also, at least partially, one of their *objects*; and that is our third general key. The new China has passed its eight years of life in a succession of fevers: the campaign for agrarian reform, the anti-American Korea campaign, the campaign for the elimination of the five types of counter-revolutionaries,[1] the Three Antis and the Five Antis,[2] the ideological re-moulding campaign, the campaign against Hu Feng and Hu Fengism, the Formosa campaign (not to mention the less important or less political campaigns, like the marriage campaign or even the campaign against the four plagues: flies, mosquitoes, rats and sparrows, etc.). Without doubt, on each of these occasions the régime pursued a definite and well-determined aim. But it may be taken as read that there was at the summit a deliberate intention to keep the country in an almost permanent state of 'campaign'. Mr. L. W. M. gave me the following explanation: 'Our people have been asleep for too long a time. They must not be

[1] The number five has a symbolic importance in China. The five types are: local bandits, feudal despots, secret agents, members of reactionary parties and organizations, and members of secret societies.

[2] The campaign against the industrial and commercial classes. See Chapter IX.

allowed to go back to sleep once more, to return to their regular routine. We must keep them, at frequent intervals, in a state of psychological excitement.' It may also be thought that these reiterated exercises, these waves of criticisms and confessions, with the feeling of uncertainty that they bring with them, make it easier to assure the meekness of the masses and easier to handle the officials. However this may be, the method is not without a certain risk. Animation artificially sustained may easily drop back into apathy; but it may also lead to excesses which may become almost uncontrollable. The stallion easily obeys the spur, but he may also unhorse the rider. Rather than slacken the pace, it may seem better to change the direction. We shall see an example of this, which is far from being the first.

I would now like, in order to introduce the subject of the *cheng-feng* itself, to go back to its origins. They go far back. We are in 1942 (according to the specialists the origins might go back as far as 1937, when a similar thesis appeared. But that would be mere pedantry). 1942 was the time of the communist government in Yenan, and it was also the great doctrinal year of Mao Tse-Tung. It saw the production of a whole volume of his collected works, the reading of which, while not devoid of interest, does not offer the charm and deep simplicity of his poems. One day, February 8th, Mao Tse-Tung was to inaugurate a school. This was, however, no ordinary school; it was a political school, the Party School of the Chinese Communist Party. To open this school Mao in his inaugural speech had to develop a pedagogic theme in keeping with this very special technical education. His speech was entitled: 'To rectify Party methods' or, in short: *cheng-feng* or 'rectification'. It was another example of what Mao himself calls jargon. In ordinary language it means: teach them to work suitably. This is the theme, that I hope to be able to put into simple language. Mao reminds his listeners that the communists are few in number. Let us reckon that there is one communist for every hundred Chinese; that would make four million five hundred thousand. That is a colossal figure. Yet all the same it is no more than one per cent, and there still remain ninety-nine per cent non-communists. The conclusion is obvious; if the communists, who are so few in number, want to exercise control they must try to prevent making themselves insupportable. But they are subject to three faults. They must correct the methods of the Party and eliminate these three faults. What are they? Subjectivism, sectarianism and finally 'the tendency of eight feet in the Party'. This picturesque phrase is borrowed from the 'eight-legged essay' which had to be written in order to belong to the mandarinate and is applied to 'mandarin manners', principally in oral or written expression (pedantry, bluff, insipidity, unintelligibility, etc.). These varied ideas could be commented on at great length; Mao subdivided them (doctrinairism, empiricism, etc.) and on occasion they have also been multiplied (commandism, etc.). But, in a word, they mean the superiority complex which is the permanent temptation of Party members, they mean arrogance. They mean too, since we are in China, 'mandarinism', a term which, here, may also be translated 'bureaucratism', which has already been included in the 'eight feet' and which, in the fresh incarnations of *cheng-feng*, will become the master-word and the master-vice.

What was, at that time, the real significance of this speech and of this first campaign for rectifying the manner of work of the Party? It is difficult to estimate. Fifteen years later, after the relaunching of the movement, we are assured that it saved China and made victory certain.[1] It is much to say. The official historian, Hu Chiao-Mu, in his manual on 'Thirty Years of the Chinese Communist Party' does not so much as mention it. What one has to admit is that the 'rectification' theme is closely bound up with the theses of Mao Tse-Tungism: the United Front, the understanding with the non-communists, the taking into consideration of the ninety-nine

[1] Party directive of April 27th, published May 1st.

per cent. Having in mind this indisputable solidarity, the importance of the *cheng-feng* campaign can be grasped, as also its permanent value. It is the reflection of Mao Tse-Tungism in the mirror of the Party; even as the various policies of the régime with regard to the intellectuals, the cults, the managers, are so many external reflections. But the communist mirror can so easily become a distorting mirror.

The specialists have noted two other *cheng-feng* movements, of lesser scale, in 1947–8 and in 1950. It would also be possible to associate with its general conception, at least to a certain extent, the San-Fan campaign (the Three Antis) of 1951, for this too was aimed against corruption, wastage and *bureaucratism.*[1]

So here we are at last in 1957.

Before its much heralded launching, the campaign underwent a phase of elaboration which it is not unimportant to follow, since in it we see at work the mechanics peculiar to Chinese politics.

The curtain went up on February 27th. But the first performance was a private view. The Supreme Council of State was summoned. It numbered eighteen hundred persons and was to sit until March 1st. Mao presented his report. The word *cheng-feng* was only referred to in passing. The title was: 'The question of the just solution of the contradictions within the people.'

Two other meetings followed. One was the meeting of the Consultative Conference, of which we have already spoken. It was to sit for a full fortnight, from the 5th to the 20th of March. Summoned later but concluded earlier, between the 6th and the 13th, was the National Assembly for Propaganda Work. This is an organ of the United Front; it unites workers on the ideological front, but is convened by the Propaganda Section of the Communist Party (the *work* of propaganda is the affair of all, but the *impetus* comes from the Party). It numbers some eight hundred persons and Mao again presented his

[1] See Chapter IX.

report on March 12th. Then the period of diffusion in depth began. The report was circulated to various organizations. Here was a further nuance which it is not without interest to mention. For the little democratic parties only their central organizations were summoned, while for the Communist Party the local organizations.[1] Thereafter, despite the universal discretion, the observers were on the alert; the diplomats informed their governments and the bureaux of experts at Hong Kong feverishly devoted themselves to solving the enigma. On April 14th Chinese public opinion was informed by the *Jen Min Jih Pao* and Soviet public opinion by *Pravda*; it was time to bring everything to a head and to summon (April 27th) the Central Committee of the Party. The festival of the First of May was propitious and at hand — the new campaign was born.

It resembled, almost detail for detail, its model.

Without doubt times had changed; there were now fourteen million communists, counting the affiliated organizations — the 'colossal figure' of four and a half millions imagined by Mao had long been passed — but all the same there still remained five hundred and eighty-six million non-communists.

The communists must behave suitably towards the masses. However, this was just what they were not doing. 'They use aggressive methods and oppression in their relations with the masses' wrote the Party directive. The article in the *Jen Min Jih Pao* used expressions that I found even more significant: they 'do not hear' — they 'do not listen' — they 'do not take the masses seriously'. The methods of the Party are always affected by the three vices — sectarianism, subjectivism and, finally, replacing the 'eight feet', bureaucratism which includes them all. The struggle against the three-headed monster must be taken up once more.

All that would have been relatively clear, had there not been a fresh chapter, which was the theory of contradictions. I

[1] This is easily explained by the differences in number of members.

hesitate to venture in this maze. Not only is the subject dry, but it is far from certain, by reason of the revisions made in the first report of Mao Tse-Tung. None the less, one must say a few words, since it was at that point that the affair commenced and it is, perhaps, from that point that it will continue. It is on that report that Mao has based his doctrinal efforts. 'Those who know' have thought, from the beginning, that the *cheng-feng* affair was of minor importance and that the really important affair, creating future perspectives, was just these 'contradictions'.

What exactly is this theory of internal contradictions?

It excites, it seems, controversy from the Marxist point of view, but not being a specialist in Marxism and having no desire to become one, I will say quite frankly that it seems to me to consist of a series of conclusions.

The first is that life is made up of contradictions. We could equally easily say of conflicts or tensions to be resolved.

The second is that these contradictions could be of a militant or a pacific character. One can fight to the death against an enemy, but one can also discuss with a friend subjects of interest or divergent viewpoints. It is for this reason that some are called external contradictions (the enemy being external) and *antagonistic*, while others are internal contradictions (for they exist within the people themselves) and are, for this reason, *not antagonistic*. They are, on the contrary, as Mao points out, stimulating.

Here, at last, is a little Marxism. After the class struggle is ended and after socialism has been established, the external contradictions will disappear. The main contradictions are within the people themselves. Since this would seem to be the case in China,[1] and as the external contradictions call for

[1] It was on this point that Mao's report underwent some marked revision. A close comparison of its text with the article of April 14th is significant.

Report: 'Like a storm, the vast class struggle of the masses in the revolutionary period has come, to all practical purposes, to an end — *but the class struggle as such has not yet completely ended.*'

Article: 'It might be said that, within the framework of our country, *the class struggle on a grand scale between us and our enemies has, to all practical purposes,*

action by the dictatorship and the others for action by the forces of democracy, would it not seem that we have only a single step to take before finding ourselves in the midst of a popular democratic China? Without doubt democracy, here considered, as Mao has pointed out, not as an end but as a means, is not to be confounded with our own conception of the word. Democracy, in this language, means at one and the same time free discussion and forceful persuasion. It does not allow for the confrontation of ideas on equal terms. It bans measures of constraint. But it brushes aside the supposition of stubbornness. What is to happen, if the constraint being brushed aside, persuasion does not succeed? Would the contradiction become insoluble indefinitely? That is the weak point in the conception of democracy in dictatorship already previously developed by Mao.[1] Despite these reservations, it is comprehensible that for the 'happy few' who had been able to make themselves acquainted with the first Mao report and were able to draw conclusions, much hope seemed permissible and many new things promised. But, from May 1st, what a disappointment! In moulding itself into the *cheng-feng*, the theory of contradictions became banal and much reduced in scale. Had there been, from this moment, a conflict of trends, a concession on Mao's part, or simply a general understanding to make use of an already proven formula as a good 'publicity stunt'?

But how, you will ask, does one pass from the subject of contradictions to that of the methods of the Communist Party?

The explanation is made abundantly clear in the editorial of April 14th (it is not found elsewhere). Internal contradictions

ended: in other words the contradictions between us and our enemies which for a long time were the most important contradictions in the country, to all intents and purposes, are resolved.'

These revisions paved the way to the thesis which was to be upheld by Chou En-Lai and according to which, among the people themselves, the contradictions could take on an antagonistic character and therefore justify brutal methods. Mao, on the other hand, considered that this could only occur in very exceptional circumstances, as in the case of Hungary (external intervention).

[1] 1949. The Democratic Dictatorship of the People.

can be of the most varied nature; in politics, in economics, in intellectual life, etc. But is not the principal contradiction that between the people and its leaders, the mutual incomprehension between them? (Read also, between communists and non-communists.) No one considers that it might perhaps be possible to resolve it by allowing the masses to choose or change their leaders. But it is concluded that the leaders must change their methods. The fundamental question (to solve each problem within itself) and the structural problem (choice of leaders) disappear when faced by the problem of attitude, of appearance and of manner. Thus, what might have been an opening towards political evolution, a struggle of conscience concerning the new conditions created by passing through the stages of socialism, a lesson freely drawn from the troubles in Hungary, is reduced to the proportions of a routine exercise in re-education and discipline in the manner of the communist party and, more especially, of its many fresh militants.[1] Large scale manoeuvres, refresher courses, together with the refurbishing of old propaganda themes; this was no longer a question of recreating democracy, it was merely a question of reading the Infantry Training Manual once more. From the very start, the new campaign was a misunderstanding and a check.

[1] '73 per cent of those members who have joined the Party after its Seventh Congress have not taken part in the "rectification" movement.' Among the members of long standing, certain have not taken part and amongst those who have done so 'some comrades have forgotten the historical experiences of the Party' — Directive of April 27th.

CHAPTER XI

FROM THE *CHENG-FENG* TO THE CAMPAIGN AGAINST RIGHT-WING DEVIATIONISTS

WITHIN forty-five days there was to be a disaster. In those few weeks the *cheng-feng* was to pass into the campaign against the right-wing deviationists. Similarly and quite logically, it was to pass from the mild form of the Chinese political campaigns — criticism and self-criticism — to the acute form — denunciation and confession.

For the moment, we are, naturally, still in the mild phase, criticism and self-criticism, which is called in communist jargon 'the unity-criticism-unity' method. We are among friends, 'within the people'. It might have been thought that the communists would reform themselves behind closed doors like the monastic orders. In fact they called on the non-communists to participate in the campaign. While one eliminates bureaucratism among the leaders, it is a good thing at the same time to eliminate mental reservations among the others; to put an end to the inferiority complex of some and the superiority complex of others. It is a two-way relaxation of pressure, but it is still 'operation misunderstanding'; one would like to think that it is the initial idea and that it is the error that will show itself to be disastrous, that all the difficulties consist of misunderstandings, insufficiency of explanations, formal incomprehensions.

In order that some should listen, explain and, should the case demand it, confess, others must say what is in their hearts, must unburden their consciences, must 'wash their brains', 'clean themselves out'.

'When you know, speak — when you speak, say everything.

Whoever warns shall not be reproached. Whoever teaches a lesson will be honoured because of it.' Significant detail: the party executive makes it clear that it is not necessary to accept criticism that is not well founded.

It was thus that the *honourable criticizing match* began. From the start 'the gentleness of the breeze and the shower' was recommended, doubtless both to spare the susceptibilities of the 'rectified' communists and to overcome the timidity of the good citizens tormented by complexes. There were to be no large meetings; only discussions in small groups. Meet among yourselves, among people with whom you work, who know one another; worker-delegates in the various enterprises, delegates of employees, co-operative delegates, groups of co-operators, employees of the same ministry; the students among themselves, the professors among themselves, and then the professors with the students, the subalterns with the service chiefs, the employees with the directors; and also the town councils in special meetings for criticism; then the Council for State Affairs, that is to say the ministers; the non-communist parties; the Industrial and Commercial Confederation, organ of the capitalists, specially summoned to a great meeting at Pekin which was to last a fortnight. Everyone met to discuss and to criticize; there was a universal coming and going. The *cheng-feng* turned the life of China upside down and played havoc with the time-tables of the Chinese. Business slackened and the administrative services were neglected. The *Jen Min Jih Pao* was compelled to utter a warning; work must not suffer because of the campaign; take your time, you will be given as long as necessary. (The necessity would soon cease to be apparent.) The Socialist University at Pekin suspended its courses so that the activist students should have time to devote to rectification; inversely, at Shanghai, the capitalists' school extended its session so that the pupils could discuss and criticize at leisure.

From the beginning an incredible paradox was apparent. A

discreet and almost confidential method had been recommended in the intimacy of small groups; the open-hearted discussions for which the limelight of large meetings had seemed too brutal were subjected to the broad daylight of the press. Every day the official *Jen Min Jih Pao* poured out whole columns of criticisms, complaints and invectives. As all this was done without classification of subject, qualification of persons or precedence of problems, the zealous archivist anxious to find his way must have the patience of the gold panner. Every morning I had headlines and crossheads spelled out to me, several passages translated, while I noted phrases down in haste, myself mindful of the advice of the *Jen Min Jih Pao* not to neglect all my other tasks for zeal of rectification. In the afternoon, luckily, the Russian paper published in China brought me in a language that I could understand weighty paragraphs taken from important articles, selected from those of the day before or the one before that. I made every effort, naturally, to get direct information; there is nothing so valuable as living sources! But those with whom I spoke, whatever their background, were themselves badly enough informed and had not much to tell me; didn't they read their own newspapers?

It has doubtless been remarked that, during my interviews with Chou En-Lai and Mao Tse-Tung, these two treated the subject with reserve; the approach of a reversal of tendency was already apparent. Mao did not say very much, but every phrase was pregnant with meaning. Later, I had a chance of considering from every viewpoint his formula: 'With a people like this, one is obliged to maintain certain limits.' Chou En-Lai had agreed to give written replies to an interview drawn up by my wife. But, out of fourteen questions, he had left blank the three which concerned the *cheng-feng* and the Hundred Flowers. This discretion was later perfectly explicable.

About this time I had had a meeting with several leaders of the democratic parties, members of the National Assembly or of the Consultative Conference. Amongst them had been Mr. Chen Chih-Chih, representing the Revolutionary Committee of the Kuo Min Tang, Mr. Ling Chi-Chun, President of the Democratic Construction Party (capitalists) and Mr. Sun Hsaio-tsun of the same party. Others also. The most important personage was Mr. Lo Lung-Chi (Democratic League), Minister of Forests, whom I met several times and who has since been accused of conspiracy. Mr. Lo Lung-Chi struck me from the start by his appearance and his evident intellectual standing. He visibly dominated the debates, as much by his personal qualities as by his position as a member of the government and as representing the most important group. But I had equally been struck by the conformity of his proposals and had the impression that he was always forcing himself to bring back to the orthodox viewpoint the replies of his colleagues when, under the pressure of questions, they showed traces of an erratic tendency. I had read in the press that the small parties were complaining of having been misunderstood and persecuted, of being the Cinderella and the Poil de Carotte of the United Front![1]

I asked:

'Are the little parties treated with more consideration since *cheng-feng*?'

'But, we have always been treated with consideration.'

'Always?'

'Perhaps; but we cannot be sure. . . .'

'What exactly does *cheng-feng* mean? What changes has it brought you?'

[1] The communists decide everything and then have it carried out by the others (*Jen Min Jih Pao* of May 8th). The communists and the democrats do not mix. . . . They should become fast friends.

At Shanghai, certain communist cadres are still unaware how many democratic parties there are in China (*Jen Min Jih Pao* of May 25th).

Author's Note: I admit that this ignorance does not seem to me to be so scandalous. I too had the greatest trouble in finding my way through the maze of little parties.

Certain senior communist officials . . . *despise* the development of the democratic parties and *threaten* persons who wish to join them. (*Pekin Daily* of May 30th, criticisms made by the democrats to the Town Council of Pekin.)

I took down word for word the conclusion that I was able to obtain; it is interesting to re-read it now in the light of later events.

'Democratic life has become broader. Liberty of speech has a more real meaning than hitherto.'

Let us go back, then, to written sources, since nowhere has the liberty of the press been more striking than during these few weeks in a country notorious for having no liberty of opinion. I asked Mr. L. W. M.:

'But if someone, in the course of criticism, expressed criticism of the structure of communism, would it be published?'

'Certainly, to-day it would be published.'

'And would he run the risk of punishment?'

'No, not at once. But a little later, perhaps. . . .'

The copious literature of criticism collected at the time gives an impression of uniformity. 'We dared not speak', the greater number of the complainants say in different tones and with varied seasonings. But now that they could speak, what did they say? For the most part, nothing. It seemed that their own boldness astonished them and was at the same time exhausted by this simple statement. They dared to say that they had not dared to speak; but what they had not dared to speak, they did not say. Perhaps they no longer knew what it was!

I noted amongst many similar phrases, those that seemed to me the most striking at the time. 'When one meets a communist one can talk only about the weather.' 'The walls that divide the communists from the masses must be broken down.' This metaphor of walls will recur frequently. At the time it was the employees of the Ministry of Public Health who used it. But what were they to do when the walls were broken down, when they could talk of other things save meteorology? One could glean minor worries, deceptive suggestions. One of them complained that sports competitions wasted too much of the workers' time, another that senior officials got improper privileges by having their families looked after free; that the Industrial and Commercial Federation had become a government office; if one thinks of the circumstances of its creation, what else could they expect it to be? The capitalists made use of a pleasing simile: 'The personnel of private capital in the mixed enterprises is like a newly married bride in former China; it dares say nothing, not knowing the character of the mother-in-law or of the husband.' But the new bride retains her reserve; to-day it is a sign of prudence, to-morrow it may be a sign of wisdom. Here and there, one finds those who deplore that China must always be inspired by Soviet models and who would like to draw more extensively on all other sources of value. But how?

Here are certain suggestions which, though secondary in nature, bear witness to a certain boldness. Mr. Shao Li-Tzu suggests modifying the administration of the sub-prefectures, now monopolized by the communists. Mr. Chen Ming-Shu proposes to dissolve the Party Committees in the schools and universities; we already know the opinion of the Dean, Ma Yin-Chu, whom incidentally I met at a reception given by the Mayor of Pekin. Powerfully built, round-faced and spectacled, he seemed the prototype of a rough, well meaning don; I think, to-day, that his attitude had at least the great merit of frankness. Finally, still in the scholastic domain, the most staggering suggestion, not so much because of its content as because of its success; that the scholarship holders sent abroad should be chosen by examination and not by arbitrary political choice. That was accorded by the cultivated and benevolent Mr. Chang Hsi-Jo without further beating about the bush. I wrote in the *Figaro* in June: first conquest of the *cheng-feng*. I can now complete my judgment; first and last.

Nevertheless, from time to time, and especially toward the end, the tone grew sharper — it was because it was rising that the end of the *cheng-feng* was near.

Mr. Lo Lung-Chi, whom I have mentioned before, took up

once more a suggestion made by the aviation students and demanded the revision of injustices committed during earlier campaigns. His colleague, Mr. Li Chang-Kang, immediately retorted: 'What are we to say if even the feudal landowners were to complain of having been unjustly treated?' This incredible hypothesis seems to have been enough to close the discussion. To-day it may be said that Mao himself in his report of February 27th had said roughly the same thing as Mr. Lo Lung-Chi, and that he had proposed to set in motion, this year or next, a complete re-examination of the work of elimination of the counter-revolutionaries, under the dual control of the National Assembly and the Consultative Conference. Chou En-Lai made an allusion to it in his speech. But while waiting, Mr. Lo Lung-Chi found himself inscribed, in his turn, on the list of eventual beneficiaries of a future revision of injustices. . .

It is difficult enough for a visitor from the West both to understand the general ferment and to find out what there is new that could justify it.

'We discuss, we criticize,' is the usual reply.

The visitor asks, naïvely:

'But, previously, didn't you have the right to criticize?'

'Most certainly! We had a perfect right.'

'Well, what has changed?' I asked, a little indiscreetly perhaps, a young 'Kanpu' of the Institute of National Minorities (Uighur and Komsomol, a future oil engineer in Sinkiang).

'Does it mean that you can speak more openly than before?'

He appeared scandalized at such a suggestion:

'But we always spoke freely before.'

The average reply might be translated in this way:

1. Before: criticism was not forbidden.
2. To-day: criticism is authorized.

On the fourth floor of the Capitalist School at Shanghai, in a suite of rooms, groups of a dozen or more ladies are chatting over cups of tea. Many of them are chic and good-looking. They are the 'manageresses', the wives of traders and industrialists. Those women who themselves work at a profession attend the men's meetings.

'What are you discussing?'

'We are saying that when we first came here, we did not understand very well what socialism was. To-day, thanks to the school, we understand much better....'

'But you still criticize?'

'We criticize.'

'What do you criticize?'

'Well, when we first came here, etc....'

After several attempts I managed, by sheer insistence, in finding a shade of criticism.

'Someone complains, for example, that one of the professors uses language too learned for his students.'

In the male groups, a dyer, proprietor of the 'Horse's Head' establishment, ended by giving me an example of critical discussion.

'We were discussing the newspaper. It has severely criticized a suggestion made at Tientsin that a rotation be established in the government between the Communist Party and the other parties.'

'Do you approve of that suggestion?'

'No, but some of us find that it has been criticized with excessive severity.'

But with this question we are drawing near to the 'turning point': the beginning of the Chu An-Ping affair....

Indeed the campaign of criticism reached its culmination on June 2nd, with a declaration made by Chu An-Ping, editor-in-chief of *Clarity — Kuang Ming Jih Pao —* during a meeting of democratic leaders. Chu An-Ping recalled that, before the liberation, Mao had promised to organize a coalition government and that, in fact, in 1948 the government had included six posts for vice-presidents and vice-premiers divided equally between communists and non-communists. But since the reorganization of the government which followed the 1954 Constitution, there was one vice-president and twelve vice-premiers, all members of the Central Committee of the Communist Party.

'Are we then incapable of being vice-presidents and vice-premiers?' Mr. Chu An-Ping asked in substance in the name of the democrats.

That was, it seems, the height of audacity. For one thing, Mao Tse-Tung himself was found guilty of 'contradictions' (it was surely his turn) — and perhaps also treated with a certain impertinence in a comparison with the great 'bonzes' and the little 'novices'. Also, the flood of criticism had now risen as high as the apex of the pyramid of power.

Finally, Mr. Chu An-Ping evolved a picturesque and very Chinese phrase — the 'one-coloured communist dynasty'.

Immediately there were protests — the workers' unions became excited — that was an unmistakable sign — the democrats themselves feared to find such imprudence amongst them although apparently on their behalf. Chu An-Ping was disavowed by his comrades in his own party and by the cell in his own paper. . . . One could smell a change in the weather. The wind had turned. It was no longer 'the gentle breeze'. After the 'beneficial shower' could be heard the rumblings of the storm.

Supplementary notes

Note A

It is strange to note that there had been no discussion on the right to strike. But this very question had been touched on by Chu Yang, Director of Propaganda, in his press conference of

May 7th, and this passage had then seemed to me new and particularly important.

'If some question gives rise to a strike, a demonstration or some other similar action (which is a very rare thing in China), then such actions could be considered as a means by which the people defend themselves against bureaucratism. . . . The Chinese people has the right to demonstrate and to strike, even as it has freedom of speech and freedom of association. No strike leader will be punished.'

We learnt later through the publication of the Mao report that there had indeed been some strikes in 1956 among small numbers of workers and students, as well as in the production co-operatives. They were imputed to the 'bureaucratism' of the executive.

Note B

It is well to remember the comic episode of the return of the leaders to physical labour. This was not a re-edition of Mussolinian fantasies, but a part of the struggle against the complexes of superiority and arrogance, to bring the leaders and the simple toilers into contact and to seek for mutual comprehension by common effort, limited however to a few occasional hours, and also, in certain cases, to encourage production by permitting the executives and the workers to compare their experience and their opinions in the actual course of work.

Also this 'physical labour' was understood in many different senses, ranging from sports to various forms of work in progress. It might be thought that Mao Tse-Tung had himself given an example when in 1956 he swam across the Yang Tse Kiang with a group of young workers, all of them good swimmers.

In the first flights of the campaign and in the enthusiasm of the month of May, the Mayor of Pekin, Mr. Peng Chen (who was, moreover, gifted with exceptional physical powers) and also the Mayor of Tientsin, the Governor of Hopei and others went to work in the workshops and on the roads. Other leaders and senior officials employed their labour, as unpaid assistants, 'under the direction of peasants, workmen, artisans and other competent professionals at such necessary tasks as rooting up weeds, digging irrigation channels, cleaning streets, clearing ditches and collecting and carting manure.' It was 'the simple life of easy monotonous tasks', but it was not every day!

The term physical labour was also extended to cover what we would call 'work in progress' in the technical sense. Thus we are told that the director of a metallurgical factory and about thirty of his colleagues took part in the preparation of the furnaces; that during a similar experiment, the secretary and the assistant-secretary of the Communist Party visited a locomotive repair shop and had been able to receive from the workers suggestions for improving methods of work; that the leaders of a provisions co-operative had spent their Sundays working in one of their main stores. . . . They had been able to confirm 'insufficiencies' in the stock, etc. . . .

CHAPTER XII

THE TURNING POINT OF JUNE 14TH AND THE CAMPAIGN AGAINST THE RIGHT-WING DEVIATIONISTS
(continued)

I. The Turning-Point of June 14th

It would be unjust to attribute the responsibility for the muddle in store to the temerity of Chu An-Ping alone. Firstly, it seemed that there had been about this time other suggestions considered to be extravagant, especially concerning economics. Chou En-Lai in his speech mentioned three of them:

A demand for the prolongation of interest for twenty years.[1]
Conversion of interest into a capital payment.
Suppression of public control in the so-called mixed enterprises.

I can say, however, that the first of these at least was mooted earlier than the *cheng-feng* campaign; it should, therefore, have caused neither surprise nor scandal. It had been formulated in January by a Shanghai capitalist and had fallen completely flat. I was told during a meeting that if it had been taken up again it was merely in the search for subjects for discussion, in the euphoria of the fashion for criticism; it was mentioned only to be refuted. I never heard it maintained by anyone, and it appeared certain that it was not the 'right-wingers' or the capitalists who had taken the initiative to revive it. As to the second, one can certainly find traces of it in the discussions of

[1] In actual fact for seventeen years from date; since interest should, in any event, run until 1962, the supplementary delay would be exactly twelve annual instalments.

the time, but it is invidious to discern in it any anti-socialist inspiration. On the contrary the authors made clear their desire to break away from their 'capitalist' status, no longer to 'wear the hat' (cf. Chapter XVII); as long as they went on receiving their annual interest, their status as capitalists was obvious. So they suggested liquidating the interest payments, and far from demanding the advantage of a cash payment they proposed that they should be given 'national bonds' equivalent to the said interest. This was really the sort of reasonable and moderate suggestion that one might expect to see appear in the new climate of free discussion (*Jen Min Jih Pao* of June 1st).

Lastly, was the suppression of public direction in the mixed enterprises ever really proposed? If it were, then it can hardly have been with much publicity, for I have not been able to find a trace of it. There were only some criticisms of the quality of the personnel employed for these duties, and the suggestion was aimed at having this or that 'public director' replaced, and not the abolition of his function.

Not only was there nothing exorbitant about all this, but it should also be remarked that the feebleness and timidity of the discussions on economic matters were in strong contrast to the liberties taken in the political field. After consulting the many and very full extracts that I had been able to collect during this period of some weeks, and after consulting references in studies by competent observers,[1] I noted a number of attacks on the Communist Party, but never a direct criticism of the structure of collective economy, a defence of capitalism, or even of a really mixed economy.

However that might have been, whether it were a question of economics or of politics, it was neither one nor another of these suggestions, or even all together, which was able by some unexpected shock to provoke this reversal. It was none of these

[1] For example, Robert Guillain, 'The Rectification Crisis in Pekin', *Le Monde*, August 1957, which gave a whole list of examples, either amusing or virulent or both.

verbal excesses which we amuse ourselves to-day in recalling. *It was nothing that could have appeared in the press.* The misgivings felt, the reversal decided upon, cannot be explained by this easily verifiable material, but only by some more secret news or records which we do not possess.

There are persons who dispute socialism; that was the major fact revealed in the editorial of the *Jen Min Jih Pao* of June 14th, which marks the turning point with the precision of a wheel track. Not only are there persons who dispute socialism but there are, in certain places, circles where it is not even discussed for the simple reason that no one dares to defend it, that no one can talk of it without being taxed with dogmatism and 'cliché mentality'! There exists what we should call an 'anti-socialist snobbery'.

This was no longer, as in the preceding articles, a question of a small clique of right-wingers. No small number was involved:

'A section of our politicians, journalists, teachers, of artists and writers, of scientific and technical workers, industrialists, merchants and students. . . .'

'Many intellectuals have overestimated their progress' (towards socialism, be it understood). This is not a matter of some insignificant persons; eminent intellectuals who think things out for themselves 'do not understand the new times'. It is the workers and the peasants who must 'put them right'.

On guard, then! This is no longer 'rectification', but the 'liquidation of socialist conquests'.

Two days earlier, the same paper had put us on our guard against a contrary error, a danger from another quarter; those responsible for insufficiencies and errors must not, it said, make use of the manoeuvres of a small clique of rightists as a pretext to evade criticism, and even to try and exact vengeance!

Forty-eight hours have been enough for this pretext to have become a worthy cause, for the knavery of bad leaders to have become defence of the régime, for a handful of rightists to have become a considerable part of the intellectual and business classes. The United Front is involved, socialism is at stake. The bureaucrats have won. Not only, to quote the words of the *Jen Min Jih Pao*, is evasion permitted but revenge is offered.

The conclusion of the article of June 14th sounds the starting-bell for the counter-campaign. The warning is given in a tone of assurance, of moderation and of disdain. It is not so much insurgents who are in question as bad pupils, it is not so much counter-revolutionaries who are to be dealt with as blacklegs of the revolution.

'A single lesson cannot in any case be enough to settle the question of position. In order that these men may pass definitely from one position to the other (the socialist position), they need many more lessons, above all when they imagine that this question has been settled so far as they are concerned a long time ago. Moreover, a lesson still remains a lesson. That is to say that the present discussion still seems indispensable, even though for certain persons it may temporarily prove unhealthy.'

II. Incidents of June 12th and Disorders Attributed to the Counter-Revolutionaries

A comparison between the articles of June 12th and June 14th (a comparison even more striking to me, since they appeared in consecutive numbers of the Russian paper *Druzhba*) makes it possible to give a date to the reversal of the campaign with a precision rarely obtainable in the affairs of this country. It is also a great temptation to try and find, within this period of forty-eight hours, whether there were not some external fact, some important circumstance, available to satisfy our taste for a definite reason. How is it to be explained? We were told on Wednesday: 'On guard, bad communists, do not use the scarecrow of the right-wing to have your errors overlooked and to intimidate and punish your critics'. But on Friday: 'What is all this about rectification?

We will deal with that later on. Everyone to the ramparts to defend the citadel of socialism!' We ask ourselves logically; what can have happened on Wednesday afternoon or Thursday morning. . . .

I was naturally very curious about this. But, also naturally, the indications that I shall now give can only have a conjectural value, as far as the conclusions drawn from them are concerned. It is very possible that the turning point of the 14th was not due to any one precise and particular fact. The verification of the 'climate' mentioned in the last of these editorials could have been a determining factor. The two articles, appearing consecutively might only have reflected contrary interpretations, contrasting themes, between which the pointer of the scales oscillated for a little more than twenty-four hours. . . . We know, for a fact, that there are diverse tendencies and even factions in the totalitarian states also, even though they do not appear, as with us, in the broad daylight of controversy and under the uncertain flickerings of indiscretion.

Having made these reserves, we may note that after all something did happen, exactly on Wednesday afternoon, June 12th and throughout the 13th. We were only to hear about it, however, in the reports given by the *Jen Min Jih Pao* of August 6th. These referred to a veritable student riot — a thousand at least led, so we were told, by the professors, in the sub-prefecture of Hanyang (Hopei). Not content with parading the streets and posting up anti-communist slogans, the students seem to have done a good deal of material damage and taken the law into their own hands in the sub-prefecture at the headquarters of the Communist Party. We were even told that on the second day after an argument with the sub-prefect, Han Mao-Lin, they seem to have 'brought ropes and wanted to kidnap the sub-prefect', in default of which they kidnapped three officials!

'After two months of investigation, the affair has at last been cleared up,' says the *Jen Min Jih Pao* of August 6th. Arrests, confessions. To-day, naturally, these excesses are attributed to the influence of the subversive doctrines of Chiang Po-Chun and of Lo Lung-Chi (see below).

Even if one cannot affirm a chain of cause and effect between these incidents and the warning of June 14th, one cannot but be struck by the coincidence. The tardy account of events is doubtless subject to caution as regards details and interpretation; but in any case it is sure that something happened and equally sure that these incidents took place in university and intellectual circles, exactly those which are taken to task by the *Jen Min Jih Pao*.

These troubles, and others more violent which broke out in the following weeks, were certainly not unconnected with the confirmation and accentuation of the new campaign against the right wing. Especially the following incidents which were noted in the press of June, July and August:

On June 17th, a bomb was thrown at the secretary of the Communist Party in the Medical School of Pekin by a twenty-three year old student, an assistant teacher in a secondary school. There was nothing to indicate that this was not an ordinary news item, yet the paper headlines it: 'The class struggle is still going on!' In this form, it is really explosive!

On June 25th, the assassination of the local communist leader at Kuntou (Shantung), and six members of his family.

On July 12th, the assassination of seven persons in the sub-prefecture of Lien Kiang (Kuangtung), attributed to a counter-revolutionary group inspired by a certain Yang Tao-Hua. The bizarre account of this affair reminds us opportunely how far the Chinese people, in certain areas, have remained backward and credulous. Yang Tao-Hua, we are told, gained an influence over the peasants by means of magic objects; swords and even gourds, which enabled him to kill his enemies within a range of twenty-five kilometres. This affair ended with twenty-nine executions. Decidedly the communist world, in this year of grace 1957, is not sparing of contrasts; the magic gourd in the era of the intercontinental rocket....

It would be erroneous to attribute too great a political

importance to incidents of this nature. On the scale of this immense country, scarcely emerging from the Middle Ages, they are of minor importance and only strike one by the very fact that the régime has succeeded in imposing, within a decade, general order.

On the other hand, it seems to me impossible to attribute them to the influence of vaguely liberal ideas which certain leaders felt themselves authorized to utter as a result of the 'rectification' campaign and, moreover, with the exception of the university riot at Hanyang, even the official propaganda has never suggested anything of the sort.

But they illustrate Mao's words: 'you have seen this people. It is not like others. One must always observe limits', and also what we have said about 'psychological progression'. . . . Also, they have certainly played a part in the general political tautness that we are noting at this moment. They might explain a a sort of *inversion of the Hungarian complex*, the leaders fearing thenceforward that liberal methods increased rather than decreased the danger.

III. The Persecution of the Democratic Leaders

As a result of the article of June 14th, discussion in fact became extremely unhealthy for those who had made the mistake of acquiring a taste for it. Those who had wished, even though by invitation, to rectify the methods of others, found themselves requested to 're-mould' their own ideology. The attacks changed targets, the hoods changed penitents.

We are now passing from the formula 'criticism-self-criticism' to the phase of 'denunciation-confession'. The persons under attack seem up till now to be few in number (150 to 200), but we are still unable to judge development in the provinces, especially in Shanghai, which is always late. We already know the rebuffs to Chu An-Ping. Other democratic leaders reply to the summons of their parties, to find themselves questioned exhaustively about their past lives, their real intentions and the like. Their houses are plastered with hand-written fly-bills accusing them of treason. Those who are ministers must appear before the National Assembly. We have already spoken of Lo Lung-Chi. Both he and Chan Po-Chun are accused of having plotted to restore capitalism and of having wanted to give wider scope to their little parties. Have they so greatly misunderstood the fable of the frog? Now we are told that they met to conspire at the famous restaurant of the Lacquered Duck, where not so long ago I once dined with Mr. Wu Mao-Sun. . . .

But there was a different reaction from Mr. Chang Nai-Chi, Minister of Food Supplies. He refuses to be penitent and lectures his companions in misfortune. Has China found her Molotov?

The *Ta Kung Pao* of June 28th, 1957, reporting his committal before the Plenary Conference of the State Council (Council of Ministers) describes him for us as 'tranquil and with his pipe in his mouth, as usual.' Giving blow for blow, Chang Nai-Chi 'counter-attacks violently. He shows himself impolite to Premier Chou.'

The discussion reported took place in the State Council (Council of Ministers) so that naturally the full text has not been published. But, later on, a special joint meeting was convened by the Party of Democratic Construction, to which the defendant belonged, and by the Federation of Commerce and Industry (the Party of Democratic Construction is representative of capitalist circles, which are grouped professionally in the Federation of Commerce and Industry). At this joint meeting a colleague of the suspect, Wang Hsin-Yuan, Assistant Minister of Light Industry, and member of the same party, delivered the full account of what had taken place before the Council of Ministers! On the basis of this report, hostile and lively enough, as one could see from the details given in the press, everyone present placed as much blame as possible on Chang Nai-Chi, who was himself absent from the meeting, either because he was not asked or because he did not deign to come. The root of the whole matter seems to be that he was being reproached for some ill-chosen words. He seems to have said, in effect: 'Bureaucratism is a more redoubtable enemy than capitalism. . . .'

For that, says the reporter, he made some 'absurd explanations' and maintained that he had not departed from the six criteria of Mao (see chapter on the Hundred Flowers). He complained, with every appearance of common sense, that they wished to judge him on a few words and not after an examination of his work and life, as he had collaborated with the Prime Minister for the last eight or nine years. 'Even if my bones are reduced to ashes, nothing anti-socialist will be found in them.'

Before leaving Pekin, I made every effort to read the article of Chang Nai-Chi on 'the walls and the ditches' which I had been told was of great interest (long extracts from it may be found in *The Galleon* of September 1957). It sets out, with well enough chosen phrases, the problem of rectification, of the 'inferiority complex' of the non-party men and the 'superiority complex' ('the illusion of being something special') of the communists. He asks, in connection with Stalin's oath at Lenin's funeral, whether 'the communists are cut out of different stuff' and answers it, to his own satisfaction, in the negative. In all that one does not see anything subversive or even anything particularly original, nor does one find the phrase which, to-day, is imputed to him as a crime. That is what makes the difficulty in this sort of affair. The views attacked never appear in articles put down in black and white and signed by their authors, but generally in conversations, and then only in the form of quotations made by their adversaries. The indictment is, at the same time, the official report.

While the campaign against the right-wing deviationists is being thus carried on, what has happened to *cheng-feng*? It is universally believed that Chou En-Lai delivered its funeral oration in his speech to the National Assembly on June 25th, after the session, as we have already stated, had been postponed for a week. But it was a funeral oration . . . of silence, and no death certificate has been issued.

The *cheng-feng* has not officially come to an end and — one never knows! It may recover one day. Nothing is definite here, every movement in one direction running the risk of breaking a delicate equilibrium and provoking a movement in the other direction. We are still within the undulatory mechanics of Chinese communism.

The Three Antis campaign set in motion that of the Five Antis, the campaigns of ideological reform and against Hu Feng were, some time later, followed by the Hundred Flowers, the *cheng-feng* has begotten the campaign against the right-wing deviationists; it might well survive it or be reborn out of it, in one form or another.

Contrary currents still mingle to-day in the depths while we only notice, here and there, stirrings of the surface with the secret hope of finding, all at once, some good logical certitude in the western manner.

Thus, certain people pretend to explain the course of recent events as a pure and simple manoeuvre. The *cheng-feng* was deliberately allowed to develop in order to provoke the opposition to make itself known and to be taken in the snare. I do not consider this version to be probable; perhaps the Chinese leaders are disposed to give it credence to a certain degree in order to justify themselves *a posteriori* and thus escape the reproof of imprudence.[1] Without going so far as the snare, there is still the simile of the vaccine, which can reveal the most diverse reactions which have not been looked for, but the existence of which is not scientifically impossible.

We, since we are Cartesians, will take things in their due order. Was there not, at the start, a real and sincere pre-occupation inspired by the events in Hungary, to which the

[1] Cf. *Jen Min Jih Pao* of July 2nd.

recent change of attitude by Chou En-Lai bore witness? Had there not been an incontestably serious effort towards doctrinal construction and adaptation on the part of the master thinker of Chinese communism? Finally, as we have seen, an alteration of this doctrinal basis and an artificial recourse to the formula of 1942?

Hence the lack of harmony and perhaps also of conviction. Has Mao not had complete faith in an affair which was not wholly his own? And the executives in an affair which was not wholly their own?

Had there not been at the start, but still more gravely later on, a conflict of tendencies, concessions and compromises?

All this, doubtless, is conjecture. What is sure is that there was, as always in China, a great deal of experiment and a double element of under-estimation and surprise. The authorities have undoubtedly under-estimated both the reactions of the various groups incited to criticism and free speaking, and also the vigour of the resistance of the communists who make up the framework of the régime; the explosive fever of the one and the obsidional psychosis of the other.

Intellectually forced, the assimilation of 1942 and 1957 was, in practice, heavy with risk.

Finally, the incidents at Hopei and the other more serious disorders which we have mentioned, though having no direct connection with the discussions and the criticism, have certainly made the leaders uneasy and counselled them to extreme prudence.

It was one thing to rectify the methods of the Party in the little world of Yenan; it was quite another thing to summon six hundred million Chinese to a vast carnival of free speaking. The miscalculations of *cheng-feng* are reminiscent of many stories and fables; the nose of Cyrano, the sore finger of Balthazar Gracian, the homily of the Archbishop of Grenada and, above all, the apprentice sorcerer, terrified by the powers that he has released. . . .

But if Mao is perhaps a sorcerer, he is certainly no apprentice. The game is not yet over. Even if the *cheng-feng* is out of date, I think that the theory of contradictions can have a longer life. We can regard its jargon as distressing and its ideology as wearisome; we can consider the use of democratic methods in one direction only as a radical vice; that if democracy is hard to establish even where it already exists, to pretend to introduce it into a dictatorship is a chimerical ambition; all this without doubt. But it none the less remains that, for many Chinese, the united theme of 'democratic methods' and 'internal contradictions' was the beginning of hope and they will not renounce it so soon.

Into this theory of contradictions, Chou En-Lai, in the course of his statement, made a brief but vertiginous incursion. It was a philosophical blitzkrieg. In a few words, he comes to the crux of the problem. He puts the whole world in agreement, conciliates all viewpoints, justifies all campaigns. Let us see:

'In the contradictions which exist among the people, the antagonistic aspect of the contradictions between the bourgeoisie and the working class exists to-day and we have still a severe class struggle independent of the contradictions between us and our enemies — that is to say, the contradictions between, on the one hand, the people and, on the other, the counter-revolutionaries within the country and the foreign imperialists.'

So: orthodox Marxism recognizes only external and antagonistic contradictions. Mao Tse-Tung affirms the existence of internal non-antagonistic contradictions. Chou En-Lai adds internal contradictions which are also antagonistic. . . .

And, to end on a note of philosophy, Mr. L. W. M. — 'Our Chinese socialism is therefore the richest. We acknowledge three sorts of contradictions — *without, of course, counting the contradictions between Chou En-Lai and Mao Tse-Tung*.'

CHAPTER XIII

A PROVISIONAL SUMMING UP—THE 940,000 SUGGESTIONS AND THE 810,000 OF THOSE TRANSPLANTED

WE HAVE seen that the peculiar logic of Chinese communism has no relation to western logic. A fresh proof is provided by the evolution of the 'campaigns' during the last six months of 1957 and the beginning of 1958.

From a western standpoint the campaign against the right-wing deviationists represented the victory of a tendency opposed to that envisaged in the 'rectification' campaign. If, in our view, the 'rectification' campaign showed a liberal tendency, the contrary deduction showed that the campaign against the right-wing deviationists marked an authoritative 'involution', a counter-movement of repressive and inquisitorial character. For us there is always a victor and a victim, a dead man (the *cheng-feng*) and a successor who condemns him.

This is not, this in fact cannot be, the viewpoint of the Chinese communist leadership. It is able to think of contraries as being entirely compatible. I said in the preceding chapter, written shortly after the turning point, that: 'the *cheng-feng* has begotten the campaign against the right-wing deviationists; it might well survive it, or be reborn out of it.' Events have justified this forecast and even gone beyond it. Indeed present-day China considers the two campaigns not only as compatible but as *complementary*. Not only are they not mutually exclusive, but they control one another. Not only can they follow one another in that alternation that I have called the 'undulatory mechanics' of Chinese communism, but they can be paired together and carried on simultaneously.

This synthesis is evident in official documents and especially in a colossal report by the Secretary-General of the Communist Party dated October 20th, 1957, especially devoted to the 'rectification' campaign, which regards the campaign against the right-wing as forming a second stage of the rectification campaign itself. Once these two stages have been passed, the report concludes, it is now time to start on the *third and fourth stages* in order to achieve complete success.

One may therefore expect, according to this report, a fresh stage of rectification (the third) and also a fresh stage of the campaign against the right-wing (the fourth), with perhaps more to come. . .

It might well be asked if this presentation is sincere. Can the rectification campaign be granted any further importance, or has it merely been invoked as a sort of alibi to preserve symmetry?

However that may be, the press continues to draw up its balance-sheet.

We are even given some impressive details of its success. It has resulted, we are told, in 940,000 counsels and suggestions. Furthermore we are informed that this figure refers only to those counsels and suggestions which have led to results, transfixing with so many steel-tipped darts, like a St. Sebastian, the three-headed monster of the 'three evil isms'.[1] Lovers of detail may learn that more than ninety thousand of these counsels concerned the metallurgical industry whereas two hundred thousand suggestions were made in connection with culture and education, of which, it is true, only eighty per cent were actually accepted.

These details illustrate very well the spirit in which the rectification campaign was launched and the limits within which it had been hoped to confine it. The door left half-open for complaints must allow many proposals of detail to pass through. The Freudian treatment must result in a 'fixation' on very secondary items of practical everyday life. It was not

[1] *Jen Min Jih Pao* of December 19th, 1957.

to be expected that the patient thus psycho-analyzed should show such impatience with, or allergy to, the régime itself or certain of its tendencies. When I noted, in my first observations, the contrast between the vivacity of the general expressions and the secondary nature of the complaints expressed, I was still wide of the mark, for these complaints, though secondary from our point of view, could still move mountains in relation to the real extent of the 940,000 counsels and suggestions which make up the 'orthodox' criticism which had the blessing of the authorities.

From our point of view the very proofs given of the vitality of the campaign show its insignificance. We are far from the hopes raised by the 'gentle breeze and the kindly shower'! One is tempted to think that, in synthesis, the 'rectification' campaign was of very little weight when compared with the anti-rightist campaign. None the less a certain importance may be given to the fact that the principle has not been disowned and that the Party remains aware of the vices and dangers of bureaucratism.

On the other hand, how has the campaign against the right-wing evolved?

It is still going on, though without increasing in scope or in virulence. There is still talk from time to time of Lo Lung-Chi and of Chang Nai-Chi; from time to time they renew their avowals but in a way that seems reticent and incomplete. And we have no information here that officially confirms that they have been stripped of their ministerial positions though in any case they no longer carry out the duties.* New names appear in the game-bag, sometimes of a sensational nature, as recently the President of the League for the Autonomy of Formosa, Hsieh Hsueh-Hung, nicknamed the 'heroine of February 28th'. However, the general impression is that the campaign is not being intensified, but that, on the contrary, it is tending towards appeasement. While the report of October 20th

* Translator's Note: Chang Nai-Chi, Lo Lung-Chi and Chang Po-Chun were relieved of their ministerial posts on January 31st, 1958.

quoted above speaks of the third and fourth stages, it may be noted that more recent writings, specifically several editorials of the *Jen Min Jih Pao*, speak only of a third stage; that is the stage of rectification. This stage, it is explicitly stated on November 23rd, can be commenced without a *transitory* bridge once the struggle against the right-wing has been terminated. Thus it is thought possible to revert without further transition or precaution from the witch-hunt to the struggle against bureaucracy.

It would, we must again point out, be vain to try to draw strict deductions or accurate conclusions from such a mass of shifting information. Doubtless it would be possible to take the documentary analysis still farther — that we must leave to the specialists — but it is impossible to go more deeply into the question when the essential element of depth is lacking or to halt what is essentially mobile. At the very moment when one thinks that one has fixed some oscillation, it has already passed onward — or been reversed.

We can, on the other hand, on the basis of all the signs and documents considered as a whole, determine to-day with a certain degree of precision the real lesson of the two campaigns. For these contradictory campaigns have, in fact, a single lesson. This has both a theoretical and a practical conclusion.

From the theoretical aspect this lesson is that the policy of assimilation pursued with regard to certain essentially bourgeois and intellectual elements has shown itself to be disappointing. The 're-moulding' has not achieved all the results desired. Each time that a liberal current has intervened, the newly converted have returned to former ways of thought or of expression. The old Adam has emerged again. . . . And every time the régime has experienced a certain surprise. The word has gone out: 'Criticism is permitted . . .' and instead of putting in the suggestion-box the formula for a new filing system, instead of complaining about the bad temper of some foreman, instead of suggesting a new edition of a Manual of Mechanics, this man or that 'asked to criticize' has decided to question, more or less openly, the authority of the Party itself or the excellence of the system. Then — 'rien ne va plus', the enemies must be tracked down, the irreconcilables put where they can do no more harm, those spirits for whom the treatment has proved insufficiently effective must be re-moulded or rather 're-remoulded'.

This situation is translated here by a new term, both significant and picturesque. After the re-moulding comes the *re-labelling*. There has been, it seems, too much haste in removing the *class label* from certain individuals. It will be necessary, according to their subsequent behaviour, to restore to them their 'right-wing docket' — to re-label them.

That surprise and disappointment was experienced by the leaders is certain. They were both the *result* of the rectification campaign, the *cause* of the campaign against the right-wing deviationists and also the *result* of this last campaign to the extent that it has confirmed the apprehensions awakened by the first one. Having said that, do not forget that we are in the country of shades of meanings. . . .

Surprise and deception, we have said; but this was by no means an entirely novel phenomenon (see, for example, the Hu Feng affair). This was no absolute revelation justifying a complete change of front. The leaders, we are told, should have understood at once the resistance that they met in bourgeois and intellectual circles. They should have made the obvious deduction, namely that a period of ten or fifteen years was necessary to assimilate the intellectuals, and this fact is presented to us as a great discovery. But the Assistant Minister of Culture had already told me in his own words: ten or fifteen years will be needed before Marxism-Leninism has been assimilated by the greater number of our intellectuals — and this took place in May, before the rectification campaign had been put into reverse and even before it had reached its climax.

Let us take note, on the other hand, that these deceptions have not induced the leaders to abandon the *suaviter in modo* and revert to the *fortiter in re*. 'Patient persuasion', 'Education'; these remain the watchwords. 'By words not by actions'.[1]

However, if forceful measures have for the most part been avoided, if there has been no wave of executions or even of prison sentences, this does not mean that the authorities have contented themselves with homilies, exhortations or even confessions. It is here that we shall see the positive, unpublished aspect of the campaigns.

In fact one cannot fail to establish an important, if not an exclusive, relation of cause and effect between the avatars of the two campaigns and a very strange episode which we may call 'the transplantation of the cadres'. This amounted to a 'return to the soil' of a very large number of cadres working in the public services or in the various departments of the Communist Party. They were sent into the countryside, to the villages, and there frequently employed in tasks of rural exploitation. In other, less numerous, cases it seems that the cadres were put to work in industry, in the factories. This was not a matter of week-end manual labour, of which we have already quoted some remarkable examples (p. 97), or even of seasonal work by schoolchildren (three million this summer) but of a long-term if not permanent settlement. The official figure given in a report of December 5th is 810,000 Government or Party workers 'who have left their posts to take up productive work in basic sectors'. More than a half of them went to agriculture and industry (so, counting their families, several million people are affected).

Such a movement could evidently serve several ends: budgetary economy, administrative decentralization, improvement of productivity and therefore also the struggle against

[1] It is, however, to be noted that there were three executions after the Hanyang disorders (p. 103) and also one death sentence after the bomb outrage at the Pekin Medical School (p. 104), but these incidents clearly went far beyond the ideological conflict.

bureaucratic excesses. From this point of view the transplantation of the cadres can doubtless be regarded as connected with the rectification campaign. None the less, it seems more probable that it resulted from a more directly political impulse and essentially from a twofold cause:

1. In order to obtain, thanks to a sort of purge, an easily controllable administration, especially within the Party, and

2. To submit to a fresh training process and 're-moulding' a certain number of intellectuals of doubtful allegiance (this term 'intellectuals' being here understood in a very broad sense, including therein employees having only an elementary culture). A stage of indeterminate duration would bring them into closer contact with the people and would doubtless allow them to retrieve their positions progressively with their education. All this while awaiting the formation in sufficient number of a class of 'red intellectuals and specialists of the working class'. The predominance maintained by the bourgeois class in the formation of intellectual youth (72 per cent according to the most recent figures) is in fact one of those problems peculiar to Communist China and a special phenomenon of the policy of assimilation.

This has caused the régime to enquire frequently into the sincerity and devotion of its young élite and to desire the creation of a reliable class of intellectuals, either by a final transformation of the élite of bourgeois origin or, better still — which will require much more time — by the eventual formation of an élite class of proletarian origin.

Those involved for the most part think that their period of probation will be short and that they will easily qualify as 'provisional peasants'. But this is by no means so sure.

We are told that during a visit to an agricultural co-operative Chou En-Lai recently met about fifty graduates who found themselves transplanted there and who asked him the fashionable question, one moreover of the greatest importance for their prospects: 'How does one become a working-class intellectual?'

The Prime Minister explained to them that this was not a simple matter and they must not think that they could reach this goal by working for a few months in the countryside. . .

'To become a working-class intellectual is not a thing to be decided by examinations or approved by leaders. It is a question of knowing if one's thoughts and feelings are similar to those of the working people and if one can devote one's whole heart to the people . . . that can only be judged and approved by the masses themselves.'[1]

And, 'encouraging the young men' the Prime Minister added:

'In the future you will be even more progressive than we are. *You will be able to enter into the twenty-first century to build up communism*.'

This encouragement was, doubtless, appreciated by those to whom it was addressed, but if it were intended to be taken literally, one must conclude that not one of them could take full advantage of it before the age of sixty. . .

However, the Chinese know how to wait.

[1] *Jen Min Jih Pao* of December 23rd.

CHAPTER XIV

THE HUNDRED FLOWERS AND THE HUNDRED SCHOOLS

THE Hundred Flowers and the Hundred Schools were not exactly a campaign, nor were they a doctrine. They were what is called here a 'watchword'. And this 'watchword' was limited, at least throughout a whole preliminary period, to the field of 'culture'. It was not until later, with the Mao report of February 27th, that it was to be given a wider application. This was not done without creating a good deal of confusion.

It is May 26th, 1956. Mr. Lu Ting-Yi is making a speech. Its subject: the policy of the Chinese Communist Party towards art, literature and science. Mr. Lu Ting-Yi is Propaganda Chief of the Central Committee of the Party. He is the usual chorus leader in all the movements of the régime. On that day he was addressing the intellectuals. He was speaking at the request of Mr. Kuo Mo-Jo, President of the Chinese Academy, who supervises in the government what we should call 'the cultural portfolios'. He did this by referring to a line of conduct laid down by Mao Tse-Tung at the supreme State Conference. Backed up by such authority, what did Mr. Lu Ting-Yi say to the intellectuals?

'To the artists and to the writers we say: "Let a Hundred Flowers bloom."

'To the savants: "Let a Hundred Schools compete." '

He explains:

'During the time of the Spring and Winter Annals (722–481 B.C.) and that of the Warring Kingdoms (403–221 B.C.) more than two thousand years ago, many schools of thought competed among themselves for supremacy. It was a Golden Age in the intellectual development of China. History has shown that when independent thought and free discussion are not encouraged academic life stagnates.'

That is surely a promising, even an enchanting, beginning? The prestige of the past, the Golden Age more than two thousand years ago; China, despite everything, did not begin in Yenan in 1942 — memories of Confucius, of Lao Tzu, of Mencius, whose schools of thought competed without dramatic conflict (China, in any case, has always had a tradition of tolerance in religion and philosophy).

To western readers it must at once be explained that a Hundred Flowers does not mean literally twice fifty; it is a symbolic manner of speaking, meaning 'many' and 'all and every' (as also, in similar phrases, ten thousand).

I think, however, that it is a mistake to translate it, as is sometimes done 'all the flowers' and 'all the schools', for 'all' followed by the definite article has in our language a sense exclusive of any exception which goes farther, it seems to me, than the meaning of the Chinese expression and, in any case, far exceeds the ideas of Mr. Lu Ting-Yi. . . .

Who then, in the distant past first formulated this elegant phrase? 'The historians and writers of the time', is the usual Chinese reply, for they do not share our taste for precision in their sources. But, putting together my conversations with Mr. Kuo Mo-Jo and with the Assistant Minister of Culture, Mr. Chien Chun-Jui and others, I have come to the conclusion that the 'Hundred Schools' was originally an expression of the historian Ssu-Ma Chien, but that the Hundred Flowers derived from a fable in which a princess dreamed that in her garden all the flowers of the world would bloom.

However that may be, the eclecticism of Lu Ting-Yi should not be confounded with that of Ssu-Ma Chien or the princess with her botanical dreams. Not only does everything not become licit, but the boundary line between what is permitted and what is forbidden is not very clearly drawn. The Propaganda Chief makes it clear that there can be no question of going backwards. There is no pity for the counter-revolutionary.

Hu Feng remains damned as such, as also an earlier heresiarch, of the name of Hu Shin; 'the criticism and denunciation of Mr. Liang Shu-Ming' remains justified, without however delivering him over to public abomination, since he, formerly an adversary of the communists, has been won over and now sits in the National Committee of the Consultative Conference. Shades of meaning. . . .

In the intellectual China of the Hundred Flowers, no one has the right to be a counter-revolutionary, but one has, to a certain extent, the right to be an idealist, in order to permit 'the free conquest of idealism by materialism'.

For those who do not find all this very clear, here is an example, that of Mr. Yu Ping-Po. Mr. Yu Ping-Po is not censurable from the political point of view. On the contrary, his faults have been literary. He must, therefore, be criticized academically. But take heed! Some criticisms have been expressed in too virulent a fashion. The critic will then be censured as well as the person criticized. Shades of meaning again. . . .

It is difficult to say that Lu Ting-Yi provides a sure prescription, an all-risks policy.

Thus the intellectuals tested by the ideological re-moulding — the literary brood scalded by the Hu Feng affair — do not seem over-hasty in rallying to the new watchword with all the fever of creative enthusiasm.

At the beginning of the year the Hundred Flowers was universally regarded as a fiasco.

None the less, the officials declared a credit balance which Mr. Chu Yang, the Assistant of Mr. Lu Ting-Yi, set out in an interview given in April and which I was able to read on my arrival in the May issue of the review *The People's China* (in Russian). There was, first of all, the field of medicine wherein was posed the very important problem of reconciling the traditional art of acupuncture with more modern methods; and here, in fact, the Hundred Flowers theme does not seem to have been without practical consequences.

In science, we are told, at least a quantitative success has been registered; more scientific literature was published last year than in the six preceding years.

In this domain the Hundred Flowers movement is associated with a twelve-year plan for the development of the natural sciences, social science and philosophy.

In art and letters, periodicals are shooting up 'like mushrooms in the rain'.

In the theatre there are many new pieces, that is to say pieces from the former repertory suitably 'rectified'.

The new 'new pieces' are mainly of a propaganda nature.

In presenting his honours list, Mr. Chu Yang makes the appropriate sacrifice according to ancient rite by denouncing both left-wing dogmatism and right-wing opportunism. What is new and really paradoxical is that this policy of symmetrical warnings should be applied under the slogan of general confrontation and simultaneous bloom....

Mr. Chu Yang has found his right-wing opportunist in the person of a certain scenario-writer who signs himself Chou Chou-Chou. In an article entitled 'Drums and gongs in the cinema', Mr. Chou Chou-Chou won a certain amount of notoriety by saying that the more one wishes to put art at the service of the masses and the working people, the less people are to be seen in the cinemas. Proletarian art means sparse audiences. Mr. Chou Chou-Chou goes as far as sacrilege; he has printed the phrase 'commercial value'....

The 'left-wing dogmatist' stigmatized is Mr. Chen Chi-Tung, author of a well-known book on the Long March.

Mr. Chen Chi-Tung laments so loudly that it might be suspected that he is trying to bring water to the mill of official propaganda, by awakening suspicions that the Hundred Flowers have a more real scope than is generally admitted.

Now it is socialist realism that is under discussion, he

exclaims! We must take up once more the old classical repertory, with amendments! We must devote descriptions to everyday life and to love! That is going too far! 'The image of our own times has become fogged, its voice muffled.'

Decidedly the problems posed by the new cultural liberalism do not seem of the easiest.

In the formal garden of Marxism, between left-wing dogmatism and right-wing opportunism, equally distant from Chou Chou-Chou who is dying of boredom and Chen Chi-Tung who is crying scandal, the least petit bourgeois of intellectuals, even when guided by the helping hand of Chu Yang and suitably provided with the complete works of Mao Tse-Tung in four volumes, must pass many sleepless nights in the search for boldness and diversity . . . in orthodoxy!

But now that we have reached the period of *cheng-feng*, all these distinctions become simple and the problem is reduced, quite naturally, to the struggle against the three 'isms'. With a sure hand Mr. Chu Yang plaits a rope-bridge.

'Our artists and our savants, by an overwhelming majority, believe in our Party and are ready to accept its guidance; what they do not like is the subjectivism, sectarianism and bureaucratism in that guidance. They are repulsed by them.'

It was, in fact, in May during the time of the rejuvenation of the rectification campaign that I had the opportunity of following, during my stay in Pekin, two of the most remarkable examples of a more liberal intellectual policy.

The first concerned traditional painting, the painting of animals, an art little subject to socialist realism and which had become to some extent despised in recent years for that very reason. The Hundred Flowers encouraged the artists to complain; they were offered as a first pledge an Academy of Traditional Painting, which was created on May 14th, 1957. The painter, Wang Hsueh-Tao, quotes some quite piquant examples of stupidity. He was reproved for exhibiting a painting of an eagle, for since such a subject could refer only to Stalin it must be treated with due respect! More recently, he had painted a picture of a flower, with the intention of offering it to an important personage. The 'Direction of Painting' found that a flower without roots was insufficiently respectful in such circumstances; the roots were therefore added to the picture by order![1]

Another story concerns a novelist whose name, as it so happens, is somewhat similar to the painter's. The young writer, Wang Meng, is to some extent a follower of the Soviet writer, Dudintsev. He has written a story entitled: 'The Young Man who came to the Department of Organization'. Though the conclusion conforms to good socialist morality: 'I will fight to the end,' the hero decides, in the struggle within the department, 'and I will keep my love hidden in the depths of my heart,' he writes of situations and sentiments which present-day literature has carefully abstained from mentioning. For this reason various official thunderbolts have descended on the author: morbid characters, a lugubrious and demoralizing book! 'It is impossible', writes the *Literary Studies* in February, 'that Kanpus (Young Communists) as degenerate as this could find positions in the capital itself', 'It is an insult to the Party.' But, on the contrary, the literary pontiff, Mao Tun, chooses to defend the bold writer. It was then revealed that the review *Literary Studies*, where the story had been published, had made the author submit to revisions and had — without the author's consent — cut a whole chapter. And here is the conclusion of the incident, both very '*cheng-feng*' and very 'Hundred Flowers': it was decided to publish the complete uncorrected text in the official *Jen Min Jih Pao*, together with the censored chapter. Thus the public could decide for itself whether to condemn or censure the author, to approve or not the re-writing.

I tried to stress the point in the course of an interview with the Assistant Minister of Culture, Mr. Chien Chun-Jui, who is one of the white hopes of the régime. The titular Minister,

[1] *Jen Min Jih Pao* of May 12th.

Mr. Mao Tun, is usually absorbed in his duties as President of the Association of Writers, and by various pontificates. Mr. Chien is a man of my own age and knows Paris, where he stayed in 1936 for an anti-fascist Congress. He gives an impression of intellectual and physical vigour and, I can also say, of frankness. The information that he gave me, especially on the problem of the illiterates, had no suggestion of bluff.

'Clearly,' said my informant, 'we do not accept the theory of art for art's sake. Art is at the service of the workers. But it is possible to serve the workers by works that have not the character of political propaganda. For example, we have our painter Chi Pai-Shih, who paints crabs and crayfish. Do you see any propaganda there?'

(True, but Chi Pai-Shih is a very old man and we know that the animal painters have complained of being treated with little consideration.)*

'Furthermore, we read translations of your own writers: Balzac, Maupassant, Flaubert. *Le Rouge et le Noir* has had a great success here. Such reading and such plays have been stimulating and wholesome for the workers.'

Take note then, Chinese Maupassants and Stendhals.

In conclusion, Mr. Chien left me with a remark which I find interesting: 'It will need a good fifteen or twenty years before Marxism-Leninism is assimilated by the majority of our intellectuals. The Hundred Flowers can assist us in this task.'

In his report of February 27th, Mao has devoted a whole passage to the Hundred Flowers, while granting no more than a couple of sentences to 'rectification'. It may be admitted that he thus wanted to reiterate his watchword, since up till then it had had only mediocre success. But it is also possible that he wished to give it a more general value, surpassing the vast but well defined domain of creative culture. He rounded off his motto 'a Hundred Flowers, a Hundred Schools' by a third adage which, as antique dealers would say, was out of period.

* Translator's Note: Chi Pai-Shih died in September 1957.

It was: continued co-existence and mutual control. The whole comprised a sufficiently exact formula for the United Front and, indeed, of 'Mao Tse-Tungism'.

While thus extending widely the theme of the Hundred Flowers, he on the other hand assigned strict limits to it. It must be thought that they had been formulated in the course of the re-writing of his report (for some of them at least, this appears incontestable). Everything happened as though he had wanted to make use of this passage, which particularly lent itself to revision, to give a general signal to halt.

It is here that Mao explains that it is possible to criticize Marxism. But it is to prove its vitality. It is always the formula: 'Criticize, so that I may refute you', 'Discuss, so that I may persuade you.' The technique of conversion guaranteed by free examination.

But the limits were to be fixed by the six criteria; each one expressed in simple form, in successive affirmation and negation.[1] The author takes pains to point out that the two most important things are: the way of socialism and the leadership of the Communist Party. It is evidently the proper thing to say: all the flowers, but in the same garden. But what is there surprising in that?

Differing from some commentators, I do not think that the formula of the six criteria has closed the jaws of the trap on the simple and naïve. What is there new in them? Has anyone even thought that he would be permitted to take up a position against the way to socialism or against the authority of the

[1] 1. Whatever encourages the union of all the peoples of our multinational country and not whatever provokes division among the people.

2. Whatever encourages socialist transformation and socialist edification.

3. Whatever encourages the strengthening of the democratic dictatorship of the people and not whatever saps or weakens this dictatorship.

4. Whatever encourages the strengthening of democratic centralism and not not whatever saps or weakens the system.

5. Whatever encourages the strengthening of the leadership of the Communist Party and not whatever leads to evasion or weakening of this leadership.

6. Whatever encourages international socialist solidarity and the international solidarity of all peace-loving peoples, and not whatever is to the prejudice of these two forms of solidarity.

Party? More remarkable, above all by its tone and its unexpectedness, is the brusque warning addressed to the small parties; it could certainly not have been written before February 27th.

'As to the question of knowing whether the democratic parties could continue to exist for a long time, that is determined not only by the unilateral desire of the Communist Party, but depends also on the manner in which the democratic parties behave and on the trust that the people will accord them.'

We are already far from *cheng-feng*. And we are far, too, from the subject of literary, artistic and scientific creation.

In this domain also the new campaign against the right-wing deviationists is no good omen for the Hundred Flowers. Perhaps acupuncture will still be lucky! But it is also lucky for Mr. Wang Meng that he has retrieved his chapter and for Mr. Wang Hseuh-Tao that he has disentangled himself from his root, for such operations would probably be no longer possible to-day. The most recent reports say that the Direction of Fine Arts no longer complains of conventional art but of inflammatory palettes. The painters meet to denounce one of their colleagues, their own vice-president, Mr. Chiang Feng, as 'chief inflamer': despite the fact that he was secretary of the communist group. Has a Hu Feng of the palette been discovered?[1] All this lends itself to irony, but it is a laboured and disagreeable irony. The favourable judgments that I have passed on other aspects of the work of Communist China, the conclusions that I have reached in this study, the aversion that I believe that I have shown to prejudices and unbalanced judgments, permit me, I consider, to say flatly how detestable I find these recantations.

I have forced myself to an objective analysis of facts, for one must always understand and one must none the less have hope.

Here we have been dealing with cyclic movements of

[1] Note also the attacks on another painter (Hsu Yen-Sun), on writers (Wu, Chou, Kuang, etc.), savants, journalists, architects, etc.

which the scale seems continually to diminish. By contrast with the *cheng-feng*, begun in confusion and completed in disorderly rout, the Hundred Flowers theme has a permanent value. The doctrine of co-existence has also an international value; Chou En-Lai and Mao Tse-Tung have confirmed it to me. We know that Mao is attached to his doctrines and even more to his allegories. This theme will reappear, without once more having to wait two thousand years, or even fifteen.

And we, while we are waiting, how are we concerned? What can we do? We must frankly express our disagreement and our deception, but not give away to sterile regrets or indulge in sarcasm. The greatest mistake of all would be to use this or that incident as a pretext to justify the absurd principle which consists in ignoring up till now the existence of a people of six hundred million, which has had its difficulties and its crises even as we have had — as, sometimes, we even still have — and which has them on its own scale, in conditions of incredible disorder and as if in a state of surfusion. The Chinese socialist state will be less uneasy, less subject to the unco-ordinated reflexes of pseudo-defence, if it does not feel itself threatened or misunderstood abroad. Our attitude can encourage, among responsible men, those who are really moved towards a comprehensive evolution, and encourage in the inmost spirit of this or that leader — for every man may become a prey to doubt — those sentiments and impulses which tend towards humanity. Particularly in the domain of culture, since that is what we are discussing, it seems to me that we could help to sustain and re-establish, by the aid of the Hundred Flowers or in some other way, liberal and progressive trends. We must give replies to the suggestions made to us, we must develop cultural exchanges and we must make great efforts to resume and multiply contacts between China and the West. In that way, it will depend on us to bring to the Chinese intellectuals that renewal and enrichment which, as they have told me, they have as much need as of bread.

CHAPTER XV

THE RÉGIME AND THE CULTS

I. The Patriotic Associations of the Cults

The Chinese State is essentially organic. All the organizations of the people's life — the social groups — must form a vast body dependent on a single circulatory system, feeding all the parts and fed by them in its turn.

No activity, no society in the general sense of the word, may remain outside this network of veins and arteries. Not only must any risk of hostility be averted, but any suggestion of indifference must be shut out.

This is true also, as we have seen, with even greater reason, for those groups who might find themselves in contradiction, on principle, with the communist state.

Such is the case with the religious cults. They are represented in the Consultative Conferences, the basic organs of the United Front.

Furthermore, the most representative of the cults are called upon to take their part in public life, either in the Consultative Conferences or by individual nomination or through the non-communist parties in the national or provincial assemblies, the town councils, etc. There is often a plurality of offices.

Finally, the cults have also a method of organization all their own. This consists of the Patriotic Associations of the faithful. Such an organization was, first of all, created for the Protestants, of whom we shall not have occasion to speak again, for they represent only a few hundred thousand persons and have no particular problems.[1] Then, in 1953, the Moslem and

[1] I had the opportunity of coming into contact with one of the moving spirits of the Protestant Association, Mr. Liu, who welcomed me at Shanghai in his

Buddhist Associations were created. On April 14th, 1957, the Taoist cult, which is a special case and had up till then been kept under surveillance, received — or submitted to — a similar organization. Finally, on June 17th, a Catholic Congress, numbering about two hundred and forty participants, of whom a third were priests and eleven were bishops, met in Pekin. Its official object was the creation, on a national scale, of a Patriotic Association of Catholics. I was told at the time that, despite the slowness of its labours, made even slower by the method of dissertation and discussion, the result could be considered certain and favourable; it was a Constituent Assembly.

However, we learnt from the press that the Congress had met again on July 15th, from which it was possible to conclude that the first experience had not yielded results. Convened for a week, it lasted a fortnight.

Finally, on August 3rd, the Constitution of the Association was formally announced, but in conditions which seem to us somewhat confused. We shall return to this point later.

One should not, in any case, be surprised at this evasion or that the régime should have encountered particular difficulty in its relations with the Catholic Church, since this cult differs from all others in recognizing an extra-national authority, another obedience than that to the communist state which grudgingly tolerates this duality. This fact had, moreover, already provoked various crises in the time of the Chinese Emperors. . . . It has been possible to recognize the seriousness of similar conflicts in the recent histories of the people's democracies. If they have been of less importance in the Soviet

other capacity as delegate of the Institute and Vice-President of the Consultative Conference. With a diplomatic background, having lived for six or seven years in the United States, Mr. Liu, with his emaciated, ever-smiling face and steel-rimmed spectacles, makes one think of Mr. Gandhi, a fact which greatly amuses him. Mr. Liu was one of the most cultured and charming Chinese whom I have had the good fortune to meet. When he came to meet me on my arrival I did not know his position in Protestant circles, so that next day I was somewhat perplexed to read in the local press that I had been welcomed at the aerodrome by representatives of the cults.

Union, it is only because Catholicism was not very strong there. The Soviet State has had, if one may say so, the luck of only having to deal with Christian communities whose heads were resident on its territory: the Orthodox Patriarch on the one hand and on the other the Armenian Catholicos, though his pontificate extended beyond the temporal boundaries of the state, and he himself came from Rumania and did not speak Russian.

What is the value of such associations? They are useful for certain administrative and material questions, the renovation and upkeep of church buildings, and the like. In this way, they are reminiscent of workshop councils and associations of the diocesan or cultural type. But, in addition, they form a characteristic mechanism in the policy of insertion which we have had occasion to define.

In this matter the value of the associations far surpasses the scope of material or administrative questions. They are indispensable cogs. Officially, each side has its own interest in them; the religious bodies in obtaining from the state the facilities necessary to them, and the state by using these centres of influence for the work of socialist and patriotic construction. Furthermore the associations and groups, in this field as in others, permit and assure the selection of 'representative persons', who are called on to make their careers in the régime (this situation would be inconceivable in the Soviet Union, where the cults, completely loyal to the régime, are not connected to it by any visible links). It is from them that are chosen so many municipal councillors, deputies to the consultative conferences, deputies to the provincial or national assemblies, who become so many living links and good conductors between the régime and the cults.

II. The Catholic Church

'A period of domestication destined to precede elimination or to make it, in fact, unnecessary'; such is the analysis of certain Catholics, who infer from it the need for reserve or for revolt.

'It is quite possible', reply others, 'to combine and at the same time distinguish between the qualities of Chinese patriot and faithful member of the Church. We should not persist in a resistance which, whatever our fervour, could be broken by force, because of our small numbers. The State will not demand of us anything incompatible with our faith. In any case, let us anticipate it loyally and try the experiment. . .'

'One cannot serve God and Mammon,' recall the first. But the others reply: 'Render unto Caesar. . . .' The eternal dialogue.

Besides this duality which confronts those who are reasonable and sincere there are on the one hand those who are regarded, here and now, as heretics and on the other the 'desperadoes' who refuse any clear analysis of the situation.

My first visit was to Mgr. Li, suffragan bishop of Pekin, whom I had met at the Mayor's reception: he is a town councillor.

Mgr. Li had three priests with him when he received me. One was the abbé, Simon Wang, already familiar to me from the book of M. and Mme. Gosset, and another the parish priest of Pekin.

The interview never got beyond the bounds of statistics and small talk.

'There are twenty thousand Catholics in Pekin, twenty-four churches, of which six are as important as this one (the cathedral is in a perfect state of repair), forty pupils in the lower seminary and twenty-three in the higher one. Priests are ordained every year.'

As distinct from other cults, the Catholic Church receives no subsidy from the state (the general rule, similar to that in the Soviet Union, is that the state, without guaranteeing any regular contribution, provides aid which varies according to circumstances: difficulties, reconstruction, restoration). The Church has its own resources, from a considerable patrimony and landed properties. On the other hand, there are still no associations of the faithful, the normal vehicle for every sort of co-operation.

It was Mgr. Li who told me of the conference proposed for June 17th.

And apart from that?

'You have, so I believe, serious difficulties?'

Mgr. Li and his friends preferred to be optimistic.

'That is all over now....'

'How are your relations with Rome?'

'Normal.'

I did not insist, for I had already read accounts of similar interviews with the same participants; furthermore, if they wanted to be discreet, I did not feel justified in infringing their discretion.

It was at Chunking that I first had the opportunity of attending Mass in the People's China. The church to which I was taken had no entrance on to the street. One had to descend, by a stair, into a court. The nave was glistening white.

The officiating priest and his acolytes wore shining vestments of dark red. The congregation was numerous (about three hundred and fifty persons, not counting small children) and fervent, to judge by the bearing of the worshippers and the number of communicants. The whole scene had a tinge of exoticism which made it the more moving; mothers carrying their babies on their backs in baskets of webbed osiers and choirboys making the collection in a net with a bamboo handle.

In the sacristy, the priest, Simon Tan, offered me a cup of warm water. He was accompanied by Father Jean-Baptiste Cheng, whom I remembered at once by name, by his duties (secretary to the vicar capitular) and from his picture in the book of M. Robert Guillain. Both were wearing blue cassocks. Father Cheng spoke French which had grown somewhat rusty (I do not hold that against him) so that I am not sure that I understood him properly. He said less to me, however, than to his earlier visitor. When I congratulated him on his good congregation, he remarked to me that it was Whitsun and that usually there were less. As to relations with Rome, he agreed that they had been interrupted.

'But we will restore them,' he concluded.

At Shanghai, a veritable centre of Catholicism, I was bent on visiting Mgr. Walsh, who is an American; he is the only western prelate still living in China, the only foreign ecclesiastic who has never been arrested.

We were in a building next door to a pretty little church in rose-coloured brick of the purest Anglo-Saxon type, with a flower merchant at the door and a cloakroom for umbrellas. The service here had none of the exotic features I had noted at Chunking, despite the fact that the servers were all Asiatic.

Mgr. Walsh may be of any age. His face is very thin and shines with serenity and character.

'When I was a young missionary in China,' he told me, 'I thought I knew and understood everything about this country. Now, after forty years, I find it very difficult to know and understand. I am not saying this because of the present régime. It is just China. . . .'

'You would hardly think it,' he went on, 'but they are the nicest people you could imagine.'

One of the stories about Mgr. Walsh is his reply to a request for basic documentation. 'There is no documentation,' he said, 'and, furthermore, there is no base.'

He had been Secretary of the Apostolic Conference, which no longer exists, and collaborator with the Papal Nuncio, Riberi, who has now left the country and lives in Taipeh, in Formosa.

'I stayed behind,' he told me, 'and I still stay because my last orders were to do so.'

In the present situation of this admirable priest, I did not think it would be proper on my part to discuss with him current problems which might have had political implications. But just one point of fact:

'I was told that two foreign priests of the four who have been imprisoned were set free yesterday evening?'

'Quite right. They are on the floor above having breakfast.'

A 'Conference' at Shanghai with five Catholic leaders, all of whom spoke French very well. My interpreters discreetly withdrew.

As this meeting had been arranged for me, I thought that its tone would be 'governmental', even 'co-operative'. I was not mistaken.

None the less, I noted that they did not deny the evidence, nor reason stupidly (up to a certain point, there was no risk). There were, however, marked shades of difference in their respective attitudes. Obviously I could not point them out here.

I spoke of the arrest, in November 1955, of the titular bishop of Shanghai, Mgr. Kiung.

'That has provoked a real crisis', one of my hearers admitted freely. 'It has calmed down a little, but the matter is not yet settled.'

'He brought a wind of revolution into the seminary. They sang and shouted, "Long live Monsignor!"'

The repression was severe and about thirty or forty ecclesiastics are still in prison (almost all Chinese). Among them is the Director of the Seminary. The interim has been assured, but with his authorization and encouragement, by another Jesuit father.

In a general way there had been, they thought, misunderstandings and incomprehension on both sides.

'Everything connected with communism seemed to us evil and devilish. We refused to have any contact with the authorities, even to get the rations necessary for the holy oils! When we were summoned, we went like deaf persons and told our beads from the beginning to the end of the interview.'

'And the communists?'

'The communists refused to relent about certain situations

and certain errors committed during the civil war. They have not always followed a consistent religious policy. We accused them of having made false propaganda against religion and of having stirred up certain ignorant persons against us. For example, when they found stage armour in religious buildings or, as in one case, an old pair of handcuffs, or grease-paints intended for the shows of the church guilds, they made the most absurd deductions.'

One must, they thought, look to the future.

'We are three-and-a-half million. It is many and yet it is few. But we have moral force behind us. The régime has tested it and has been surprised. But it could, none the less, put an end to us.

'It would be easy to stir up the ignorant masses against us.'

They were all inclined towards the socialist régime and the present policy, and believed in the good faith of the authorities. They developed with various degrees of complaisance and conformism themes already familiar to me. They were encouraged by the trends apparent in the 'Hundred Flowers' and the 'rectification' campaign.

But — and this point seems to me essential — they were determined to remain disciplined in religious matters. They recognized the authority of the Vatican. The excommunication of the Abbé Li of Nankin proved a touchstone. They deplored this and thought that the authorities at Rome had been incompletely informed and had not understood the situation. But the measure having once been taken, they felt they must submit themselves to authority and regard it as valid. 'Rome has spoken . . .' — at Shanghai.

None the less, the Abbé Li was to take part in the Pekin Congress. This gave rise to a certain uneasiness. But the opinion prevailed that the Congress was largely a meeting of a laic character. It was strongly opposed, I was later to learn, by certain Catholic circles. But I, for my part, cannot solve this point of canonical interpretation.

They certainly did not represent the majority of Catholics.

But their position seemed to me so much the more interesting, especially in view of their protestation of fidelity to the Vatican.

Finally, I had the opportunity of meeting, separately and in private, two priests whom I knew to be worthy of trust.

In these interviews, details of which I cannot transcribe, I found the two intermediary schools of thought about which I spoke at the beginning of this chapter.

One of them stuck to certain practical and positive rules:

'We have been able to put an end to a certain number of petty irritations; for example, concerning the administration of the sacraments in hospitals, where there have always been difficulties with the time-tables and the rules. Many buildings, too, should be given back to us. Also, the Catholics must be excluded from everything that concerns birth-control propaganda. We ask that the teaching of Marxism — to which we are not opposed — should be done in a manner and in terms which respect our religious feelings. Later, we shall bring up again the question of certain schools. There are already Koranic schools. But if the Church is eternal, the life of the Church goes on from day to day. . . .'

The other school is more apprehensive about things spiritual:

'Good types of men hold back from entering the priesthood. They fear they will be forced to act against their conscience.'

Communications from abroad are few. One of these men would say freely:

'We have received no instructions *forbidding* us to. . . .'

And the other:

'We would very much like some explanations, a line of conduct. We have received no instructions *authorizing* us to. . . .'

One would say:

'I know very well that some people already look on me as a heretic. None the less, we are not "people's priests". We ask you to avoid hasty and unjust comparisons. In France, too, you have had your Concordat.'

And the other:

'I know very well that some people doubt my patriotism. However. . . .'

One of them would feel ready to say:

'I see no reason why the religious authorities should refuse to. . . .'

And the other:

'There is no reason why the state should not appreciate. . . .'

The first would willingly conclude with the famous invocation:

'My country right or wrong.'

And the other, who loves Claudel:

'All is easy, oh my God, save to resist Thy will.'

The imprisonment of Mgr. Kiung and the other ecclesiastics still in prison undoubtedly plays an important role for both these schools. The first hopes that, with goodwill, everything will be arranged and appeasement will follow. The other is reticent in committing itself until this mortgage of sorrows has been lifted.

To employ the language of the courts, one sees in it 'a nullifying impediment' and the other a '*non possumus*'.

The second Catholic Congress was held between July 15th and August 2nd, that is after my departure from Pekin, so that I could only follow the development of the problems involved through the Chinese press. But, in the meantime, two factors complicated the situation:

1. In July the Vatican disavowed the nomination of Mgr. Chang Shih-Liang as Capitulary Bishop of Shanghai, and
2. The campaign against the right-wing made the position more difficult and made a real and serious agreement unlikely.

The *Jen Min Jih Pao* of August 3rd confidently announced — that the Patriotic Association had been formed, and — that the Congress had decided to break off all 'political and economic' relations with the Vatican.

This very precision proves that even the most won-over Catholics had not accepted a breakage of 'religious' relations and that they did not envisage the creation of a schismatic Church.

The newspaper reports made clear, on the other hand, the existence of a real opposition. They showed, it is true, that one hundred and eighty participants were ready to criticize the stand of the Vatican in the affair of Mgr. Chang Shih-Liang. But this very fact shows that a quarter of the Congress had refused to take this view, a minority of some importance in a meeting of this kind where the irreconcilables had not come. On the other hand, among the hundred and eighty, it is far from sure that the regrets or criticisms that they expressed went as far as insubordination. We have already seen a similar situation in connection with the excommunication of Mgr. Li.

Finally, the Chinese press refers to some most courageous stands in favour of the Vatican and even against socialism. Their authors, however, would later have admitted their errors....

The information, admittedly limited, which we have at our disposal only confirms me in the impression that I had already formed that there are sincere and disciplined Catholics who are willing to try the experiment of co-operation with the régime. But it also appears that, even on the most favourable hypothesis, this experiment will have to be postponed to a later date. That the Association should have been officially set up is of no great significance in itself, since such an attempt could not be allowed to end with a setback. But one may have doubts, to-day, of the effective character of this achievement. To arrive at a *modus vivendi* acceptable to both sides, the authorities must be in a frame of mind and must be ready to make certain pacifying gestures that are not in accord with the prevalent rigorist tendencies.

This problem of the survival of the Catholic Church in China is one which has caused me the most serious preoccupation in the whole of this study. But there also I return to my leitmotive. I am convinced that the establishment of better relations between the People's China and the Catholic states could only, by its mere existence and by a general atmosphere of understanding, favour the future position of our co-religionists, whose courage and whose trials deserve not only our warmest thoughts but also a clear and efficacious effort in the field of action open to us.

CHAPTER XVI

THE RÉGIME AND THE CULTS (*continued*)
THE OTHER CULTS

III. Moslems and Buddhists

Since they were not dependent on any external authority, Mohammedanism and Buddhism did not present so formidable a problem to the communist state, nor was their incorporation into the régime accompanied by any apparent crisis. Did this mean that it did not encounter, and does not encounter, any resistance? Quite the contrary. But it was a purely passive resistance, in other words a reserve rather than a resistance. The dates seem to indicate that there were difficulties at each stage of the organization. It was only in 1953 that the Associations were created on the pyramidal system, some time after the experiment made with the inoffensive protestants. It also seems that co-operation is not yet general in all the provinces. On the other hand, it was only in 1956 that it was decided to create, at the same time, a Moslem and a Buddhist seminary in the capital. The concordance of these decisions confirms the existence of a general policy.[1] It is reasonable to assume that the intervening period served as a time of tests. In encouraging the formation of new ministries on the national level, the State made a great concession and ran a risk: we may be assured that it considered this risk carefully, after having been able to verify the extent of its indoctrination and the loyalty of its dependents.

As a general observation, it must once more be stressed that the interest shown by the régime in the Buddhists and

[1] Followed, we recall, by the creation of a Bureau of Cults, directly responsible to the State Council.

Moslems goes far beyond the scope of the policy of 'incorporation and unity' as we have defined it. Beyond the opportunity for tightening the control that it exercises over them and strengthening the support that it receives from them, the régime finds a double advantage of great strategic value in the organization and co-operation of these religious groups. On the one hand, it is a means of exerting influence on the large national minorities which it can make use of profitably to increase its authority in the outlying regions, such as semi-autonomous Tibet and, on the other, as we have had occasion to note, it draws a far from negligible advantage in its international public relations when dealing with other peoples of Buddhist or Moslem religion.

IV. Islam

The problem of Islam has an entirely original aspect in China, since all the Moslems without exception belong to the national minorities. There is not a single Moslem of pure Chinese stock. The Moslem cult is none the less organized as a cult in the prescribed manner, with a Patriotic Association and the like. But the Moslems are represented in the United Front and on the Consultative Conferences exclusively as members of the national minorities.

There are ten million Moslems in China, the results of different settlements that the Chinese ethnographers class together on a religious basis in a common group that they call 'hui', but which modern ethnography would class partly in the Turki group (Uighurs three to four million, Kazaks about three hundred and fifty thousand, Kirghizes about a hundred and fifty thousand and small groups of Uzbeks, Tatars, etc.) and partly in the 'hou' group (Hui Tzu or Tungan four million, Pantai five hundred thousand). It is naturally impossible to determine the exact number of practising Moslems as distinct from Moslems by origin. The genial Mr. Ta Pu-Sheng assured me that they all practise their religion. I tried an experiment when visiting the Institute of Nationalities, where

I was shown the halls where they, Moslems on the one side and Buddhists on the other, practise their devotions.

'How many pupils belong to one or other of these two religions?' I asked.

'About half and half.'

'But do they all practise their religion?'

'No, I don't think so.'

'What is the approximate proportion?'

'It is not possible to find out since, when they meet for prayer, no one may disturb them.'

In their status as a national minority, the Moslems benefit from a remarkable privilege. They have, despite the monopoly of education, their own schools.

As far as their material life and their financial relations with the state are concerned, their situation is the same as that of the Buddhists and seems modelled on the Russian system. The replies that I received at Pekin and at Sian seemed an echo of my recent conversations with the Mufti of Tashkent and the Archimandrite of Zagorsk.

'The state does not provide any regular subvention, but it comes to our aid when needed, if we have any difficulties; in cases of restoration, for example. . . .'

It is not the same for the Catholic Church, which receives no subvention. The ecclesiastics with whom I discussed this subject told me that the Church has its own resources especially in landed property. Is that the only reason and is this exception definite? Might it not, on the contrary, be because the Catholics are not yet 'organized' like the others and that the creation of a Patriotic Association, the normal channel for economic aid, will bring them into the general picture from this aspect also? The supporters of co-operation with whom I talked told me of church buildings which need to be renovated and restored, which leaves one to suppose that the authorities who were, moreover, responsible for their disrepair could be called upon, in a perfectly normal manner, to take the charges upon themselves.

I had the opportunity of meeting leading Moslems and of visiting various establishments. I must say that everywhere I found evidence of an enthusiastic attachment to the régime.

At Pekin, Mr. Ta Pu-Sheng, member of the Town Council, as had also been Mgr. Li, received me most graciously in the outbuildings of the mosque. He wore the black skull-cap of a priest and had a long, sparse Chinese beard. He was an imam, President or Vice-President of the Patriotic Association and also deputy in the National Assembly. With him was the Secretary-General and another Vice-President or Assistant Secretary-General (one never knows very well), both wearing the white skull-cap of the faithful. They offered tea, naturally, but by Islamic privilege with sugar; the only exception that I noted in the course of my innumerable discussions. The hall where we met, the great mosque shining with cleanliness and vivid paintings and the garden, all gave a wonderful impression of meditation and repose.

Mr. Ta Pu-Sheng is a refined and cultivated man. After having expounded to me the general problems of which I have given the gist in the preceding paragraphs, he dilated upon the great liberty which the present régime allowed for the exercise of religion.

'But didn't this liberty exist before?'

'It was certainly recognized officially, but it was somewhat illusory.'

'So everything is better to-day. Then, too, isn't there the new seminary?'

The moment had come to open a doctrinal conversation. Was there not a contradiction between Communism and Islam? Mr. Ta Pu-Sheng had noticed nothing of the sort. Between the materialist philosophy of history and the spiritual explanation of the universe?

Last year, the Mufti of Tashkent had replied to a similar question:

'I am a man of religion and I know the religious texts well, but I am not competent to express any opinion on Marxism.'

The reply of Mr. Ta Pu-Sheng amounted to:

'Communism is atheist, but the practice of religion is free.'

A last question:

'Are there any practising Moslems enrolled in the Communist Party?'

The reply, which I asked to be repeated, was affirmative. In these Franco-Chinese dialogues through an interpreter one is never sure to have been properly understood, nor to have understood properly. There are Moslems and Moslems, Communists and Communists.

During a chance excursion near Pekin we stopped in a village where a building of unusual architecture had attracted our attention from the road. It was a sort of pagoda with a green cupola; but it was, in fact, a little mosque with a Koranic school, for this village had a partly Moslem population. It was there that I met the Moslem teacher with a white skull-cap, Mr. Yu Hua-Ming, owner of the little dog which guarded his chickens.[1] A group of children surrounded us and watched us amiably. They were not so advanced as those in Canton, for the words France and Paris meant nothing to them. All of a sudden an open-faced youngster burst into a peal of laughter and all the others joined in. What did he say? They translated with some embarrassment: 'He said you have a big nose.' On leaving, I asked Mr. Yu to point out his best pupil to me, so that I could give him a miniature Eiffel Tower as a souvenir. It was the same boy; but he had taken to his heels. . . .

At Sian, at the end of the little Street of Science and Culture, I was quite astonished to find myself in a Moslem quarter. The impression was completely African. There was a group of children here too, but these had been warned and applauded the French visitors. At the entry to the park in which was the Great Mosque (there are fourteen in the city),

[1] Cf. p. 51.

the Imam, Mr. Yu, with Chinese beard and black skull-cap, welcomed us. With him was a layman in a beige Chinese tunic, waving a black fan. I have forgotten his name. He was the representative of the Council of National Minorities. He too was a Moslem, a deputy in the National Assembly and a member of the Democratic League.

Along the avenue which led to the great pagoda with its low ceiling of carved wood with Arabic inscriptions, we saw advancing along the foot of the steps some men in white skull-caps. They were the seminarists. There were about twenty of them. Their pay is from thirty to forty yuan.[1] Mr. Yu was their professor. There is also a little seminary with fifty pupils. There are two teachers, one Koranic, one part time for Chinese (their pay is from fifty to sixty yuan). According to the usual custom, it is the Moslem families who pay for the needs of the establishment, but the State gives aid in certain circumstances.

'Till now,' the Moslem deputy explained, 'the Sian seminary has been the most important in China.'

'But now you will have one in Pekin?'

'Yes, it is being organized. We have asked for teachers from Egypt.'

I noted this detail, which I had not been given in Pekin.

'Our brothers from Pakistan and Indonesia have come to pray in this mosque.'

Public relations!

'How many Moslem deputies are there in the National Assembly?'

'From forty to fifty.'

'Are any Moslems communists? Do you know any Moslem deputies who are members of the Communist Party?'

'Certainly, I know several.'

I had no reason to doubt his words, but I persist in thinking that they could not refer to practising Moslems but only to Moslems by race. However, why always ask this question,

[1] One yuan — about 3/-.

since I am convinced that there is an incompatibility between religious practice and membership of a party which is dogmatically atheist? (Unless communism in the Chinese manner includes, on this point, an extreme latitude of which I do not think it susceptible.)

In fact, the replies are by no means unimportant.

It is not the fact that matters, for I know there can be no doubt of it; it is precisely the reply itself, its embarrassment, and, eventually, the error that it involves.

When I had put a similar question to the Chinese Catholics — I am speaking now of Catholics entirely devoted to the régime, amongst them Mr. Wu himself — they all exclaimed with a single voice there could be no question of a practising Catholic being a militant communist, for neither would the Church admit him, nor would the Party. They considered, no less definitely, that the same was valid for other religious cults.

When I had put this question in the Soviet Republics of Asia to Moslems equally devoted to the régime, they had replied simply that they knew of no such cases, without speaking of any incompatibility of principle.

How did it happen, in these conditions, that men like Mr. Ta Pu-Sheng, the Sian deputy and others also, had answered with different and, to say the least, evasive formulas? This was worth investigating.

I in no way charge them with deceit. Not only was this alien to their standing and to what I knew of their character and the impression I received from my conversations with them, but what object was there in doing so? What would be the practical result? How could they hope to beguile me into so great an error, if they were really conscious of the error and if they were intentionally trying to falsify the evidence?

The only explanation of their attitude was that they were not really convinced of the spiritual incompatibility between Marxism and religion. They think that there can be, in certain cases, Moslem communists. They can believe, in all good faith, that they know them. They may fear to say something hurtful to communism by making any statement without due consideration and even when they were clearly aware of a doctrinal analysis universally accepted, it still seemed to them perfectly simple and they replied without equivocation and without anxiety.

They know very well that the Communist Party is atheist and they admit it when the conversation turns that way, but does that atheism seem to them anything more than a sort of laicism? They know that the communists are atheists, but they do not know exactly *why* they are and *why* they cannot be otherwise.

Would they be very astonished to hear one day that, by the hazard of some new 'rectification' campaign, atheism would no longer be in fashion in the Party?

This proves beyond all doubt that communism has penetrated their spirits more as a régime than as a doctrine; but it also proves that it has penetrated deeply, that the cogs of political thought and religious thought interlock easily in a single brain, and that even Moslems whose religious constancy is sure do not find any real difficulty in 'ideological co-existence'.

To go back once more to the jargon of the Party, we are faced here with an example of non-antagonistic contradiction. This is, undoubtedly, at least partially a result of the suppleness of Chinese communism and of the support occasioned by the successes of the régime, but it is at the same time a sign of the psychological success of these methods. Let us go further: it is a sign of the success of communism among Moslem populations. This success is a fact. I can even add that this success does not seem to me entirely linked with the special methods of the Chinese leaders, for it had appeared to me incontestable in the Soviet Union also, although the problem there was posed in somewhat different conditions.

There are some who will doubtless reproach me for too much subtlety and for giving too much importance to replies dictated by prudence. The uniform explanation of terror seems to them necessary and sufficient.

I recognize that the starting point of these comments is doubtless only a detail, but it confirms and illustrates many observations, both various and concordant. Furthermore, why should the Moslems be more terrorized than the others, seeing that it is they who are the most tactfully treated?

Even if the Moslems have not, like the Catholics, both a support and a subject of conflict in their external hierarchy, that is no reason to suspect them of being lukewarm in their religious feelings, since these in other circumstances provide a source of fanaticism. Constraint has not prevented the Catholics from stiffening their opposition at Shanghai and still does not prevent the wisest of them to-day from prolonging and renewing interminably the discussions at Pekin which should have been ended in a few days.

How is one to explain, in a simple and conformist manner, why Moslem fanaticism is sometimes unleashed in so formidable a manner against democracy (which is philosophically not hostile to them) and is so anodyne towards communism (which is philosophically hostile to them)?

The *cheng-feng* has given rise to complaints from the most varied milieux and from all kinds of men, who have not all been simultaneously stricken by an access of foolhardiness; but I have not up till now heard of the slightest Islamic complaint. . . .[1]

The psychological success of communism among the Moslems seems to me so clear that it presupposes, over and above the causes that we have already mentioned, some real affinities. Doubtless the Moslem appreciates in the communist the spirit of control, the personal discipline, the faith that seems analogous to his own (it has already been noted that Moslems easily accord their sympathy to religious persons

[1] In the most recent reports I note, however, that the headmaster of a Moslem secondary school at Shanghai is mentioned in a group of fifteen right-wingers (*Jen Min Jih Pao* of August 27th). This isolated case seems a mild one and not connected with religion.

practising another cult) and, finally, an impulsion which helps him to turn towards the future. Without doubt, some points of resistance exist, but I think that they are more imputable to the oldest, that is to say the least active, amongst them and are due more to attachment to customs and traditions than to any dogmatic preoccupations.

The younger and more dynamic amongst them are, on the contrary, grateful to the communist régime for having freed them from certain feudal survivals which have been falsely regarded as religious traditions (this feeling is particularly acute in the Soviet Republics. It has also been expressed to me in China, but with much less insistence, which may be explained by the fact that here in China archaic ways of family life were not peculiar to the Moslem group alone).

The West can commit two cardinal errors in its policy towards Moslems.

One is to think that they will gain the support of Moslem peoples by maintaining and respecting leaders and institutions of a feudal nature, instead of helping them to take their part in the way of the future, which includes the emancipation of women, the suppression of polygamy, liberation from excessive family autocracy and the like.

The other is to think that an essential religious antagonism to Marxist philosophy constitutes an insurmountable barrier against the penetration of communism.[1]

Let us take note of, and draw conclusions from, the trust and one could say the lack of constraint with which the Chinese leaders have encouraged Islam not only within their own territory but also in external affairs. This proves that they reckon to gain great advantages from fraternization between Moslems of the communist countries and Moslems of the non-communist countries and that they have no reason to fear a risk of external contagion or the scarecrow of pan-islamism.

[1] Events in Syria, which took place after these notes had been written, seem to me to confirm both one and the other of these conclusions.

V. Buddhism

If it is possible to make an approximate estimate of the numbers of Catholics and Moslems in China, a similar attempt would be quite useless for the Buddhists. Buddhism is a semi-official religion in China, but the Chinese have never been deeply religious by nature. Prayer is not carried out in the congregation of the faithful and it is difficult to distinguish the onlookers from the devout, the occasional worshipper from the sincere adherent. Then, too, Buddhism has been 'assimilated', and mingled with metaphysics, Confucian formalism and moralism. For the visitor Buddhist excursions are more adapted to archaeology and sightseeing than to political observation.

My first visit was to the Lamaist cathedral which, although restored with Tibetan propaganda in mind, gave an impression of disorder and abandon. Here there was no ceremony, no one to welcome us, no tea or conference. We saw only the seventy-five foot high Buddha, swathed in an enormous robe of soiled yellow silk, and three countrymen in long surcoats, of poor and rakish appearance, who multiplied their prostrations while uttering short exclamations which were incomprehensible to our interpreters.

Later, we made an equally unprepared visit to the principal Buddhist temple, the Kuang-Tse, which on the contrary was the perfect example of an interview; one could see immediately, as the Russians say about churches, that the temple 'was working'. This time we were not long unperceived. There soon appeared before us a personage in a blue Chinese tunic, the Vice-President (laic) of the Patriotic Association, deputy in the National Assembly and member of the Democratic League. Soon a conference was organized around the tea-table; we were joined by another Vice-President, also a deputy in the National Assembly, but this time a religious personage in a grey robe, also a third in a saffron robe, the principal ministrant or shall we say the doyen of the temple.

My hosts flattered and at the same time embarrassed me by lauding French science and culture in the field of their religion. It seems, they told me, that French savants are preparing a monumental bibliography of all that concerns Buddhism in all countries and at all times. I agreed eagerly but could give them no enlightenment on the subject.

The usual questions produced the usual and conventional replies; the state provided aid but not of a regular character, the Association had been founded in 1953, a seminary had been in course of organization since the previous year. I learnt that it had been suppressed since the liberation. Where, then, had religious instruction been given in the meantime? In the parishes. (This reply reminded me of that made by the Orthodox clergy at Zagorsk. Before the re-establishment of the seminary the clergy had been recruited thus 'in the parishes'.) On the whole, all went well. All went better than before the present régime.

'Communism is no way incompatible with Buddhism. The Communist Party is atheist, but religious practice is free, etc. . . .'

On the test question; are there practising Buddhists who are at the same time militant members of the Communist Party? I obtained from my three hearers, questioned separately, three differing replies:

The lay Vice-President. 'Yes, there are, but not here. In the south Buddhists are members of the youth organizations.'

The clerical Vice-President: 'Yes, there are, but amongst those who practise their religion at home. They are not to be seen in the temple.'

Finally, the doyen: 'Yes, I know one of them in this parish.'

I was taken to see the important library of sacred books printed on wood and then the 'treasury' of the temple. They showed me there the treasure of treasures, the tooth of Buddha or rather a miniature gilded pagoda in which this relic is enclosed. It is only exhibited on certain dates. I learnt that before 1954 it had been preserved in a real pagoda of which I saw a photograph, and that it was twice the size of an ordinary tooth.

Do not think that I am digressing into mere frivolity! There are only four similar relics in the world, four teeth of Buddha. Furthermore, it must be known that one of them is in Heaven, another in the Palace of the Dragon, that is to say in the sea. There remain, then, one in Pekin and one which is preserved in Ceylon.

The Buddhists carry out political acts of sacred courtesy with these teeth of Buddha. This one has just passed a period between 1955 and 1956 at Rangoon. Around the miniature pagoda are still smaller pagodas arranged like a guard of honour, containing other relics; one offered by the Dalai Lama, another coming from Ceylon. Public relations!

I was to have other opportunities of meeting religious personages, principally at Chunking, in a temple built near a pass decorated with grottoes containing Buddhist sculptures which I was told were thousands of years old. At first sight it made one think of a formal rock-garden, perhaps because a café stretched as far as the pass. In another building we admired, as in the Green Jade Temple of the Clouds near Pekin, the five hundred disciples of Buddha, less ancient but none the less ennobled by three hundred years, painted in vivid colours and lined up as if on parade.

The café that we had seen and before which one passes from one temple to the other does a thriving business. It was filled with lively parties, men, women and the inevitable children scampering between the tables; they drank, smoked, laughed. It was not there by chance, nor was it an anti-religious demonstration. It was the main industry of the community. The waiters who served were themselves 'bonzes'. It was not only a café but a sort of vegetarian brasserie. For religious reasons meat could not be served, but well prepared vegetables, with the outward appearance of meat dishes were, so the restaurateur-monks told me, particularly appreciated, above all on hot summer days, even by agnostic gourmets.

The temple is the centre of a community of three hundred monks. All do not work in the restaurant; many carry on various trades, tailors, Chinese doctors and the like. The monks are fed and get about ten yuan (about 30/–) a month. We were to see, later, many other Buddhist cafés, especially around the pagodas which surround Hangchow; some of them are stylish and tourists take their ease in deck-chairs with tea and refreshments. Their food is not always strictly vegetarian.

I asked here and elsewhere, naturally, my usual questions. No one saw the slightest incompatibility between Marxist materialism and spiritual religion. As to Buddhist communists, they do not exist among the priests; as to the ordinary worshippers, perhaps. No one can tell. The old bonze of Chunking added a personal note to the classic dialogue: 'I think that there is much resemblance between Buddhism and communism. For communism works for the whole world, and Buddhism says that all the world will be saved.'

VI. The Taoists

I was hoping for a chance of making the acquaintance of the Taoist cult, to meet these suspects and perhaps rebels, in any case the 'bad pupils' of the United Front.

It was not so easy as one might think and the experience, moreover, was to prove disappointing. I was told of a temple near Chunking, but it meant a day's journey to go there and back and a ten kilometre walk in each direction. We decided to wait till Shanghai.

In the heart of the picturesque Chinese city we discovered, quite by chance, a Taoist temple. On one side it faced and merged with the street, its statues ranged along the way, and on the other it backed on to a closed garden decorated with kiosks and sculptures. It was, they told me, the Temple of the Under-Prefect. This translation, I was later told, was open to dispute and it would have been more exact to say 'the Temple of the Dignitary'. But I prefer the first name. Without lacking in the respect that religious thought or philosophy inspires, I must say that this Temple of the Under-Prefect was an extraordinary bric-à-brac, a hallucination of delirious slop-shop keepers.

Amid a number of other miscellaneous figures, amongst them a general on foot, some red horses and the like, the effigy of the Under-Prefect reigned supreme. He was, I was told, a virtuous and popular administrative personage of the times of the Ming dynasty. Daubed in rose colour and tricked out with a long black stage beard, he was in every way similar to a character in a Chinese opera, the *Walk in the Tortoise Park*, which we had seen at Sian, and who was, moreover, also an under-prefect or dignitary who excited the admiration of the public by his knowledge and his legal scruples.

On one side of the altar one saw the Under-Prefect deified at the side of his wife and on the other placed under the tutelary effigy of his aged parents. Several devotees came to light joss-sticks and pieces of bright red candle before the images, the colours red and rose having, it seems, the predilection of this strange cult.

At the time of our incursion, the monks were seated around a table, occupied in prayer. They continued imperturbably without paying the slightest heed to our presence nor to the horde of children that we had attracted and who were racing in from all sides. There were five monks, but I was to learn that only two were attached to the temple; the others had been invited for the celebration of a feast.

One of them, with a crown on his head and dressed in a brilliant red surplice seemed to be directing the rites. Each of them had a cup of tea and a saucer of grain beside him. Under the direction of their leader, they alternated responses to the prayer with the beating of bizarre instruments, little bells, hammers, little cymbals.

I was at last able to have an interview with one of the monks in the calm of the garden where we sat down on a bench.

Stripped of his sacerdotal ornaments, he appeared in

worker's clothes and a cap. But the moment of originality was past and the moment of truth was disappointing.

The old banal replies disturbed the peace of this devout spot.

The Taoist cult was satisfied with the solicitude of the authorities. There was no regular subsidy from the state, but there was occasional aid, notably for this temple which had just been restored. It was later confirmed to me that the temple had been shut up for a long time, doubtless not solely because of the need of restoration. . . . The Taoist Patriotic Association had been founded on April 14th. . . . They had just chosen delegates to the Consultative Conference . . . the buckle of assimilation had been closed. The page of insurrection had been turned. The war of Lao Tzu would not take place.

PART THREE

CHAPTER XVII

ECONOMIC STRUCTURE — THE MIXED ECONOMY — THE REVOLUTION AND THE MANAGERS

WE MUST distinguish three sectors of Chinese economy:

Agriculture,
Petty trading and crafts, and
Industry and commerce.

It is only in the third category that the 'problem of the managers' has been posed and has been settled. The so-called 'mixed economy' which, however, does not deserve this appellation, is also to be found in this category.

I. AGRICULTURE

Chinese agriculture is now almost wholly '*kolkhozian*'. Collectivization is, in fact, from 96 to 97 per cent effective (besides the collective farms, there are only a very small number of 'equalized' estates and naturally the State Agricultural Enterprises).

The present situation has been preceded by intermediate stages, the intricate study of which has to-day only a retrospective interest. The Agrarian Reform, which included the division or, more exactly, the 'equalization' of land, has not been applied throughout in a uniform manner.

A distinction must be made between regions, especially those where division was carried out before the law of 1950. One must also distinguish between the various categories of landed proprietors and 'rich peasants', that is to say those who employed hired labour. In a final phase, the co-operators were still partially remunerated in proportion to the lands over which they still held rights (40 per cent), which gave a real effect to these intricate distinctions. To-day, all that is out of date. Every worker within the co-operative is remunerated according to a points system similar to the Russian system of the '*trudoden*', that is to say according to his work, whatever may previously have been the size of his lands or the nature of their expropriation. Inversely, the landed proprietors and rich peasants, more or less expropriated or 'equalized', have been permitted, after a period of purgatory, to return to the bosom of the co-operative.

Chinese agriculture is, then, to-day completely uniform and collectivized. The Chinese system resembles, detail for detail, the Russian system. No special consideration has been granted in favour of the former land-owning classes; indeed they have been treated with especial severity. They have now disappeared, as classes.

It is, moreover, to be remarked that in China one is never brought face to face with 'landowners' or 'rich peasants', whereas it is easy enough to meet all other categories of the population.[1] A certain number of landed proprietors who lived in the cities and who already had, or were able to find, other activities have been definitely sundered from the land. The others have accepted their new destiny and, like the former rich peasants, have been submerged in the mass. They continue to live in their houses but, even if these are far from spacious, they have been called on to take in tenants who pay no rent. In the country the situation is very different from that in the towns where the rights of property have been respected.

Why this difference?

I have been given many and complementary explanations:

'Landed property', said one, 'is feudal property — distinct from capitalist property. The class of landed proprietors has

[1] I have been able, after asking for them, to meet some persons of this type in the Kolkhozes, but only those who previously had small estates.

not shown its devotion to the régime, in contrast to the "national bourgeoisie".'

But, above all, there is the question of efficiency.

'The landed proprietors and rich peasants are not skilled groups. They have not contributed any experience or irreplaceable techniques to agriculture.'

Will agricultural collectivization be any more successful in China than in other countries? We can only note that this method of exploitation has found here conditions relatively favourable:

> Because of the small scale of stock-breeding which is usually the weak point of all collective or co-operative economy, production deficiencies in this sector are not apparent (the Chinese kolkhozians freely admit that pigs raised privately by the peasants are a little bigger than those raised in the co-operative).
>
> Because of the smallness of the cultivable area per head (one or two *mu* per person)[1] and the extremely archaic methods of cultivation, exploitation in common is more adaptable to large scale enterprises (irrigation: theory of the 'oriental society') and to the only conceivable improvements, doubling of harvests, crop rotation or new methods of cultivation.

Despite the relatively favourable conditions for the adaptation of collective exploitation to Chinese agriculture, it may be taken as a fact, based on a whole series of indirect observations, that this method still meets with strong resistance. The very fact that the executive bodies of the co-operatives are made up exclusively of communists (or at least as far as my experience goes), though it makes verification of these observations difficult, strengthens the probability, for if the kolkhoz method had really entered into the life of the people it would not be

[1] This figure is the result of my own observations. According to the Minister of Agriculture, the general average is five persons per hectare, that is to say two and a half *mu* per person.

Without doubt the co-operatives which I visited were cultivating land of more than average worth.

necessary to bind it up so drastically with the political organization.

Peasant mentality has similar traits the world over. In China, as elsewhere, the man of the soil has a natural taste for property and for a certain autonomy. But it seems that here the discontent is less against the principle of collectivization itself than against the 'insufficiencies' of the accounting system, which is necessarily complicated, difficult to understand and liable to error and injustice, and against the intervention of persons from outside the area, whether they be 'foreigners' called in to control the co-operatives or agricultural technicians who are accused, rightly or wrongly, of not knowing local conditions, customs and traditions.

II. Petty Trading and Crafts

Crafts and petty trading should logically be studied together, because of the similarity of the social and economic standing of the persons involved. It is diametrically opposed to the field of 'large scale trading', comprising industry and the more intricate methods of distribution which, for their part, are treated in common, and where the 'contract with the bourgeoisie' is in force.

In contrast to agriculture, the crafts and petty trading sector is not completely socialized, but it is now in course of socialization. Three types of organization may be distinguished:

1. Co-operative organization, which is really socialized;
2. The type of organization wrongly described as mixed economy and which is also a socialized organization in a transitional stage, and
3. The free organizations, which are in a state of expectation.

Co-operative Organization

The co-operative method is widespread in craft organizations and is intended to include the whole field, as is already the case in agriculture.

The analogy goes far, for the crafts co-operative, of a highly socialized character, is a real craftsmens' *Kolkhoz* (what is known as an '*artel*' in the Soviet Union).

The crafts co-operative and, in the majority of cases, the commercial co-operative, as they exist in China, are very clearly differentiated from institutions of similar name in France. In France the co-operative is, as an entity, very similar to an ordinary enterprise of free economy; it participates in the normal hazards of free economy, it can suffer losses as well as make profits, and the financial situation of the individual co-operator is susceptible to equivalent variation.

If, on the other hand, we consider a co-operative on the Chinese craft co-operative system, we see that the situation of the co-operator is very similar to that of the salaried employees:

1. They receive a remuneration which is not subject to reductions (it is for the most calculated on a piecework basis).

   They can receive a supplementary payment based on a share of the profits, but this variable part of their remuneration is proportionately insignificant and is scarcely different from the usual value of a tip.

   Thus workers working nine hours a day and paid from 40 to 80 yuan a month (to take a specific example) have one thousand yuan available at the end of the year for distribution among sixty-five persons, that is to say the average value of a week's work — much less than our thirteenth month.[1]

2. A second trait of state socialism is the diminution of executive duties. If the co-operative were really an enterprise, distinguished only by the internal relations bebetween co-operative associates, the role of the director would be important and he would have to be paid

[1] In the example quoted, the proportion of the profits distributed was one third, the remainder being earmarked for various communal improvements or social benefits.

accordingly. But, in fact, the director is here no more than a book-keeper and is paid as such, on an equality with the average worker, and far below the most skilled worker (in the example chosen, the director receives 40 yuan a month, while the craftsmen doing the most delicate work, paid on a piecework basis, earn twice this amount: 80 yuan).

3. These characteristics are easily explained, in the majority of cases, by the fact that the State is the sole provider of raw materials and the sole purchaser of finished products, that it fixes the buying and the selling prices and the margin of profit. Even in those enterprises which, by their nature, cannot be subject to this rule — as, for example, the case of a photographers' co-operative working in the Park of the Imperial Tombs near Mukden — I have observed that the condition of the co-operators was roughly equivalent to that of the salaried staff.

As to merchants' co-operatives these deal with activities which fall either in the sector falsely called 'mixed economy' or in the sector which is still free, and in consequence they have similar characteristics.

Pseudo-Mixed Economy

The term 'mixed economy' is frequently used in small-scale trading for an organizational structure which has nothing in common with that term and which has, furthermore, the disadvantage of creating confusion with the term 'mixed economy' when applied to the industrial and commercial sectors (almost equally incorrectly, as it so happens).

This is, in fact, commission trading. The traders sell products provided by the State and are remunerated on a commission basis, the buying and selling prices being controlled. It is, therefore, a completely socialist economic form, including a variable remuneration (similar, in fact, to payment by piecework). The size of this variation is itself reduced in all cases where there is a certain regularity of demand.

The Free Sector

Finally, many traders and craftsmen belong to the free sector. They occupy the lowest position in economic activity; they are:

1. Fixed traders, all those who do not obtain their supplies from the State, that is to say mainly the little bars and restaurants (establishments of a certain importance having been given an organization which will be described when dealing with large-scale commerce) and those also whose premises are improvised and are scarcely worth describing as shops. Finally, according to the towns, those who have not yet been dealt with.
2. The countless street-traders; traders who install covered trays along the pavements or in doorways (these usually belong to the family of the porter, if not the porter himself), little perambulating restaurateurs who walk about with their little bells and portable stoves and make it possible for workers of every kind to get a meal at any time and in any place; hawkers of objects of everyday use or seasonal production, from matches to soap, from umbrellas to straw hats, and the horde of artisans and handymen of all kinds, upholsters, locksmiths (it seems that Chinese keys have a strange tendency to get lost or broken), and preparers of food at home.

This swarm of shopkeepers in miniature and street-traders (a hundred and sixty thousand for the city of Shanghai, compared with twenty-six thousand 'large concerns' and thirty-six thousand commission traders), is explained by the conditions of life peculiar to China, especially the difficulty of transport. It gives the streets so picturesque an appearance and is the citadel — shifting and undermined — of capitalism. These penny scrapers with their bamboos on their backs, their portable stoves and their little bells, uphold the last vestiges of the prestige of free economy.

Thus it is easy to understand in China what seems so incredible when it is said abroad; the attraction of the socialized sector for those who are not yet part of it.

All the world wants to be socialized, that is to say to become to some extent an official.

Here as elsewhere the materialists (Marxists) give idealistic reasons, the idealists (the bourgeois) material reasons.

The pedlars whom I questioned at Chunking certainly replied: 'We want to serve the state. . . .' but they also said: 'The sun is strong here; it is better in the shop across the way. . . . Sometimes we have to stop work because of illness. . . .'

This is a sort of pro-state Chinese Poujadism.

To conclude: the world of petty traders and craftsmen is partly socialized and partly free. But the free part is bespoken to socialism and is a willing partner. This sector, which might be called free, being composed almost exclusively of individuals or households not employing anyone and not making anyone else work, could hardly be considered as a 'contrary sector' in a socialist economy.

On the other hand there does not exist in these branches of Chinese economy any sort of intermediate stage — and the division between the sectors does not correspond to any organic idea. Assimilation is only a question of time and material resources. In Russia, similar elements remained for long outside the economic régime. They were, it is true, far less numerous.

How could this swarm of irregulars and nomads of Chinese economy be admitted to the serried ranks of the public sector? The very idea is enough, at first, to make one shudder. It will not take place in a day. There will be professional regroupings. As soon as transport has improved or rather, in many districts, when it begins to exist, when the Chinese people begin to lead a less harrassing life, then these most archaic methods of distribution will lose a great part of their reason for existence. One can, thenceforward, foresee a certain 'settlement' of these nomads and, with the development of industry, a regrouping of professions which for many will be only a return, since many of them have become street-traders because of unemployment. Will Chinese trading thereby lose some of its charm? Will the mode of life which is now so pleasant in form be compromised? It is far from sure.

If the transformation is carried out with patience and flexibility, if a sufficient number of distribution centres are retained, and personal interests taken into consideration, then success is not impossible. It will be made more probable by the spirit of discipline of which the shopkeepers have just given an example (intricate bookkeeping, respect for the prohibition on the sale of antiques, etc.) and to which is allied a strong tradition of business integrity.

III. Industry and Commerce

It is in this category that the really original aspect of Chinese economy is to be found.

The State Sector

Let us first note that in this category there exists a sector, originating in the state, which is becoming more and more important; this includes the new factories set up by the state and the large stores (similar to the Soviet Univermag), as well as those factories or businesses which have been confiscated outright as belonging to the bad bourgeoisie which, as we have already noted, is known as bureaucratic capitalism.

This state sector would not deserve any particular notice were it not for the diminution of powers of the executive — as in the case of the co-operative workshops. Not only is the wage scale very wide (workers from 30 to 100 yuan a month) but the principal director is paid on an average 170 yuan — less than the Chief Engineer (220). This diminution, whether applicable to remuneration alone or whether it also indicates the weakness of the work provided, will pose a problem for the economy. It also marks, as we shall see, the generally inferior standard of the directors of state enterprises when compared with directors of capitalist origin.

The sector formerly private (and not confiscated) must be clearly distinguished from this purely state sector.

The Mixed Economy and the Policy of Repurchase

It is here that the economic contract with the business classes is applicable — even as, in the United Front, the political contract with the intellectuals and the bourgeoisie in general is applicable.

It is this condition of industry and commerce that is defined by the term mixed economy.

Here too it is by no means accurate or at least it is so no longer.

There is no mixed economy, for there is no real link between private initiative and the state. There is no special type of economy which could be intermediary between free economy and socialist economy.

There is to-day a completely socialist and state economy, with:

1. Machinery for the partial indemnification of expropriated owners, and
2. The retaining of capitalists in executive positions (managers).

Because the Chinese have proceeded in this field with a certain flexibility, because they have known how to handle and to preserve the capitalist executive groups, many persons abroad have thought that they were not firmly convinced communists and that they would not go to extremes. There too the formula 'communism in the Chinese manner' created an illusion. But those who believed in this illusion have convinced no one save themselves.

The Chinese leaders have, from the start, put their cards on the table. They have proclaimed their aims openly and, furthermore, the process that they intended to follow in order to assure their complete realization.

This was the three point formula:

Utilization
Limitation
Transformation

corresponding to three stages, of which the last has now begun.

Utilization means: we shall make immediate use of the economic material, in the widest sense of the word, in the state in which we find it, while avoiding any disturbances. Hence the necessity of retaining provisionally both the men and the organization.

Second stage: limitation, that is to say limitation of the capitalist organization by limitation of profits. This was the method called: 'To each of the four horses his share of oats.' A quarter of the profits of the enterprise went to the government as a revenue tax, a quarter to a social and cultural guarantee fund, a quarter to a reserve for the expansion of production and, finally, the last quarter to the capitalist owners.

Third stage: a fixed interest rate of 25 per cent was substituted for the limited participation of the capitalists in the profits. This 'transformation' was accomplished by the end of 1955. The interest was to run normally until 1962. Afterwards, what was to happen? There would be no question, in any case, of recovering the capital. The interest, normally, would cease. There would, none the less, said Mao Tse-Tung, be a 'tail'. It was thought that the interest would continue to be paid, in certain cases, either wholly or partially, for a further uncertain term, to certain capitalists, probably those who could not work in the enterprise and who would be in straitened circumstances. The matter has not yet been finally decided.

A Shanghai capitalist has suggested that the interest payments be prolonged for another twelve years. In the heat of discussions which made up the 'discussion and criticism sessions' of the *cheng-feng*, this suggestion was taken up again only to be refuted and rejected. All the industrialists whom I questioned and, at the school for capitalists, all the wives of industrialists and merchants declared themselves against it.[1] When I asked, a little maliciously, if the motives which led them to reject the prolongation of the interest payments after 1962 should not logically lead them also to renounce current interest payments up to that date, they simply replied: 'The government has considered that a period of transition is necessary.' We shall see shortly how that docility and conformity is to be explained.

Let us consider the first point raised: compensation for the expropriated. They would receive firstly a variable sum, amounting to the 'quarter share of oats' derived from profits in the years 1952 to 1955.

Secondly, seven annual payments of 5 per cent, that is to say 35 per cent of the capital on the basis, I was told, of a three-party (state-owner-workers) assessment which seems never to have given rise to dispute.

Such a system could be regarded, as in the story about the 'half-full' or 'half-empty' bottle, either as a partial compensation or a partial confiscation.[2]

[1] See Chapter XI.

[2] 'It is a confiscation of the greater half' Mr. Jung Tzu-Cheng, an industrialist of Tientsin, would have put it. As in so many other cases his proposals are only known because of their refutation by the workers in the course of counter-criticism (*Jen Min Jih Pao* of June 17th). According to the same source, the assessment of goods for the interest service would have been generally reduced, inversely, as he points out, to the assessment which the tax authorities would have made for their purposes. The total amount of capital involved in this system should be reckoned at 4,500 million yuan and would thus have been reduced to 2,200 million yuan. This last figure is in fact the one given me by officials of the Bureau of Administration of Commerce and Industry. It can be seen that the amounts in question are not of great importance in the whole — less than

The second stage of the so-called mixed economy involves: the retention of the capitalist owner in his executive post, in his own house or in his own shop.

Is his situation secure?

There are no texts to say so, but everyone admits that it is — that there will be security of employment as long as the capitalist manager can carry out his duties, and a reasonable pension at the usual age.

What does he gain?

The reply is always: the same emoluments as before.

If we go more deeply into the matter, we shall see that this reply is only partly accurate.

In fact the 'transformation' stage, which came into operation in 1955, has not changed the salaries of the executives.

But these have, almost always, been reduced in the course of an earlier period (1950–1). The owner had then 'accepted', in order to take his share in the general effort, a more or less serious amputation which brought his salary to the head of the usual scale which, in China, is a wide one. This was, as we have already shown, one of the results of the campaign of the 'Five Antis'.

The owner-directors whom I saw received a monthly salary of from 200 to 400 yuan (30,000 to 60,000 francs). Before 1951, some salaries had been as high as a thousand yuan or more. But though reduced their salary is:

> slightly higher than the salary for comparable posts in the state industries (the director of an important factory usually makes about 170 yuan — less than the Chief Engineer (220));
> The highest in the enterprise (same comment as above).

The owner-director is now doubled with a director nomi-

350 milliards of francs. From the same official source, the number of capitalists working in the mixed enterprises would be about 700,000, which represents a very low annual average of interest payments per person (about 25,000 francs). But all these figures are to be treated with reserve.

nated by the State.[1] Both have the title of director; one is the director of 'private capital', the other the director of 'public capital'. They both welcome one at the doors of the factory, with smiles on their lips, but it is not hard to discern infallibly at first glance which is the 'private' and which the 'public' director. Despite this apparent equality, the 'public' is in fact an assistant-director and at the same time a controller (they sit in the same office); he receives a lower salary calculated, this time, on the basis of state executive salaries.

I wondered if the 'public' director were not placed next to the 'private' director in order to learn the job and thus be able sooner or later to replace him, thus cutting short the period of transition. My observations, however, lead me to believe that this is not so. In no case has the public director seemed to me adapted or destined to the administration of business; he is rather, I should say, a controller with a twofold task. He can control the owner, but he also controls the work of the workers. He maintains the discipline which, in the previous period, was usually slack. He concerns himself primarily with social questions and personnel. He is there to make the workers understand that the enterprise belongs to the State and that they must refrain from sabotage or fancies, which the feeling of working in an insufficiently socialist manner might earlier have excused. The director of public capital, who always belongs to the Communist Party (though this has been denied, I have never seen an exception) plays, in reality, the role played in the army by the 'comrade political commissar'. *He is the political commissar of the shop or of the factory.*[2]

To conclude, there is not, or rather there is no longer, any

[1] This rule is general throughout industry. In commerce a part only (about a third) of the shops are placed under the régime of mixed economy and provided with a state-nominated director.

[2] Even in this limited field, it seems that some amongst them have only a very restricted sphere of action. This function would seem to have served principally to 'find a job' for a certain number of demobilised soldiers. The industrialists and merchants do not, as a rule, complain of their 'public director'; but there are exceptions since a political report tells us that a certain Pan Wei-Liang, a representative of private capital in an office equipment shop and 'an enemy of socialist reform', strangled his colleague (*Jen Min Jih Pao* of August 8th, 1957).

mixed economy. One might have been able to speak of it when there still was distribution of profits. But one can no longer speak of it now, since the capitalists receive only compensation in the form of fixed interest payments and those who carry out the duties of directors are remunerated on a salary basis.

And now, one last question.

Is the capitalist satisfied, and why?

All the capitalists whom I asked declared themselves satisfied and put such hyperbole into their professions of faith that most people would have seen in them either the effects of constraint or of remarkable irony.

In reality, as I have mentioned before, the materialists here make use of idealism — and the idealists of materialism.

It may doubtless seem astonishing that the grace of Marxist ideology has simultaneously descended upon all the dispossessed financial élite.

With the dulled understanding of a bourgeois idealist, I have always hitherto rejected this explanation which, however, may in certain cases be at least partially true; also, no one was kind enough to provide me with others, save those which I could have easily enough have thought of myself.

That is also the advantage of a trip like mine; I did not only meet this or that factory director whom no one had any reason to choose from amongst the most disgruntled, and who had been able to rehearse his statements till they were word perfect but also to meet, at the top of the tree, men willing to give me explanations of intercontinental value.

And, finally, there is Mr. L. W. M.!

Thus the question is no longer: why is the capitalist satisfied? but: why shouldn't the capitalist be *relatively* satisfied?

The principle of a 35 per cent compensation, the interest payments clearing the capital, shocks the legal traditions of a country where there are expropriation tribunals (yet has not the most recent legislation introduced some novelties in this field?).

But the Chinese capitalist has other comparisons before his eyes.

The landed proprietor who had no executive functions has seen his lands expropriated without even the shadow of compensation; no one has ever proposed to him that he should gain more than the simple peasants and it has only been after a long delay and wearisome trials that he has been able to attain, in the bosom of the co-operative, the position of an ordinary wage earner.

The capitalist industrialist or merchant is therefore relatively at an advantage with his 35 per cent, which he is free to deal with as he wishes (he has, furthermore, the right to withdraw any capital contributions which he has been able to make since the advent of the socialist system). He retains, also, an interesting and relatively well paid job.

This same capitalist has, on the other hand, often bitter memories of the pre-communist period, which was accompanied by inflations and difficulties of every kind. More recently, he has passed through the trials of the 'Five Antis' and even if he has not been personally affected by them, the memory of them leads him to accept his present lot more philosophically.

Finally, he has already passed through the experience of two successive stages, that of limitation and that of transformation and, in the majority of cases, *the more socialist stage has proved the more favourable to him.*

Doubtless the phrase 'participation in the profits' would seem closer to capitalism; but it has often only meant disappointment. I was able to investigate several instances of revenues due to participation, and I noted that either there had never been any profits at all or that the capitalist received less under this system than he did from the payment of fixed interest.

In a general way, working conditions had become very hard for the non-socialized enterprises.

Certain owners would say: 'Since socialization, the workers

work with enthusiasm', which Mr. L. W. M. translates: 'In the the period before socialization the workers had become insupportable.'

The owner goes on: 'Since socialism we have had planned economy. Production is improving', and Mr. L. W. M. completes: 'In a system where the State controls raw materials and market outlets, it is essential to take one's place in the State economy.'

Thus it is by no means impossible that, over and above his patriotic feelings or his ideological conversion, the capitalist-manager, his fortune reduced but renewed, his salary lessened but guaranteed, with a political commissar responsible for good labour relations, finds in his present job that most precious of boons in all countries and above all in communist ones — peace of mind.

It is like a Chinese version of the fable of the shoemaker and the financier. The financier manages his finances without anxieties, even as the shoemaker cobbles his shoes. It is the shoemaker-financier.

The man who handles money detests money even as 'the captain hates the sea'.

We experience a certain surprise in visiting the school for capitalists and noting that, after some months, all the pupils without exception are convinced of the excellence of the régime.

But this is easier to understand when one knows that, symmetrically, there is also a sort of counter-school.

While some are teaching the capitalists the benefits of Marxism, others give courses and lectures to the workers, explaining to them why it is necessary to compensate the owners, and why the owner is still seated in his director's armchair, and to make them understand these anomalies.

If the owner is reserved towards socialism, so also is the worker reserved towards what remains of capitalism in the socialist city.

Hence this correlated pedagogy.

The owner will be so much the more disposed to let himself be convinced since he desires that the worker, on his side, should also be convinced.

And then, there is the future.

The communist leaders have wisely avoided eliminating the executive cadres and thereby saved themselves from damages, that would doubtless have been irreparable, to the fragile and inexperienced economy. They take much care to remind us, and back their views heavily with quotations, that this assimilation of the 'managers' was expressly provided for in the Leninist doctrine.[1]

On their side, the capitalists have salvaged their jobs as managers, not only for themselves but for the generations to come....

'Children no longer want inheritances....'

This phrase, frequently used, makes one smile at first. One thinks of an excess of zeal — or of hypocrisy.

But soon it does not seem so surprising.

In a collective economy, the possession of goods does not lead to prestige. The satisfactions procured by money very soon reach their limit once personal requirements are satisfied. The case is quoted of a great industrialist who bought, with the approval of the authorities, a Soviet automobile; but this was an event, almost a fairy-tale[2].

The structure of socialist economy being established to the

[1] 'We can and must combine methods of ruthless repression towards "uncultivated" capitalists who will not even admit state capitalism and who continue to undermine Soviet measures by speculation, corruption of the poor, etc., and methods of compromise or "repurchase" with regard to those cultivated capitalists who are moving towards state socialism and are capable of letting it form part of their lives, who are useful to the proletariat as intelligent and experienced managers of very great enterprises, which effectively assure the provisioning of tens of thousands of persons.' Lenin: *Left Deviationism and the Bourgeois* (Complete Works, Vol. 27, p. 311).

[2] A Western technician who had not wished to leave China said: 'I am poorly enough paid, since I get only 400 yuan a month — infinitely less, moreover, than my Soviet colleagues who are not so highly qualified. But what have I to complain of? I live well on my salary. I have a house. I have a staff of servants whom I pay 45 yuan a month, which is good. My expenses for food amount to 60 yuan. I ride a bicycle.'

summit and descending little by little towards the base of the pyramid, capitalism can exercise no attraction for the young élite. Where will they take the latest models of free economy? To the pedal-taxis or the open-air street kitchens?

So that to play the game, to carve out a career in the régime, avoid being earmarked as an heir and the son of a rich family.

The leitmotive 'the children no longer want inheritances' is rounded off by a very Chinese phrase: 'They do not want to wear the capitalist hat.'

But they too progress, through instruction and technique, towards the real purposes of the élite.

In the universities and higher educational establishments only twenty-eight per cent of the students are the sons of workers and employees. Even this figure is recent and the students concerned are only in their first and second years. . . .

Seventy-two per cent of the higher cadres now in course of formation are of bourgeois origin.

Therein lies, doubtless, the main justification of the 'contract'. It is also the explanation of one of the principal problems facing the régime.[1]

IV. Communism in the Chinese Manner (*concluded*)

The study which we have made of the structure of Chinese economy will allow us to appreciate the originality of Chinese communism, but also to reduce it to its exact dimensions. 'Communism in the Chinese manner', yes, if it is a question of atmosphere, tone or methods. But no, if it is a question of doctrine. The conclusions which we have reached in this field are therefore in accord with those which we have reached concerning political life and organization and the main features of that organization.

We must avoid a too frequent misunderstanding.

We start off too often with the idea that real communism is Soviet communism; thence we conclude that everything that

[1] See Chapter VII.

differs from the Soviet model is either less communist or not communist at all.

It is an imprudent deduction.

There is, in the Soviet Union, communism *plus* Russia; in China there is communism *plus* China.

We see in Chinese communism features that are not Soviet. Can we see there features which are not communist?

In agriculture, in the minor branches of trade and crafts, in the major branches of commerce and industry, in what way is the doctrine amended or misunderstood for a single minute?

There does not exist in China a sort of *mitigated* communism, a real *mixed economy*.

We have seen that this term means, somewhat vaguely, in one instance the remuneration of merchants by commission and in another and more important instance a system of repurchase and indemnification and a means of recruitment.

There is not, or is not any longer, any association between public capital and private capital; this formula has never existed save in a transitory form. It has now been abolished.

Finally, if at the foot of the scale there are a fairly large number of wretched intermediaries and petty craftsmen who have not been integrated into the system, theirs is no more than a state of expectation, and even if it is prolonged beyond the term foreseen, it will in no way modify in any essential feature the well-designed outline of an authentically socialist economy.

If I continue to insist on this lesson, it is because I have myself passed some time in China with an illusion common in the western countries — and in others. Often personages of the communist countries of Europe have spoken to me in this way:

'The Chinese do not realize their luck. They have the advantage of not having fully socialized their economy. They must keep their flexibility, halt half way along the road; that will spare them the troubles which we know so well, of having to take a few steps back.'

During the first weeks of my trip I had never wearied of asking my Chinese acquaintances, especially those belonging to the democratic parties, this question — but I never even got an echo. And in fact, the question is scarcely relevant. It is, moreover, remarkable that in all discussions that followed the movement of criticism in the *cheng-feng*, the political predominance of the communist party has been questioned with courage and not without risk, but not the system of collective economy. Communism has been criticized as a party, but not as a doctrine or a system.

'Communism in the Chinese manner' is Karl Marx gone to school with Confucius; it is a lesson in courtesy, patience and prudence. But there is no hesitation in its step, no uncertainty in its thought, no sign of a new construction or a bold synthesis for the future.

Not only do the Chinese communists never question their doctrine as far as their own country is concerned, but they concern themselves with its extension abroad. They consider that the methods they have used favour this expansion, that they lessen certain resistances and give communism a more attractive aspect which, to some degree, aids its propaganda.

It is interesting to note that this argument is laid down in the conclusion of the directives explaining to the workers the procedures employed in regard to the owner-capitalists and of the policy known as 'repurchase' of the enterprises.

'Every year China welcomes a growing number of foreign guests, amongst them a certain number of representatives of the bourgeoisie. If socialist transformation is carried out correctly in China, this can, to a certain extent, help overcome or lessen their fear of socialism. By that, and to the same degree, the world communist movement will encounter less resistance. Thus the application in China of the policy of repurchase for the peaceful transformation of capitalist enterprises appears absolutely indispensable, even from the international viewpoint.'

We find here the true originality and shrewdness of the Chinese communist leadership; having handled financially its own bourgeoisie in a tactful manner, it is at the same time preparing psychologically to handle ours.

CHAPTER XVIII

THE OUTLOOK FOR CHINESE ECONOMY

I. Agriculture

One must begin this enquiry by first considering the essential point. Chinese agricultural economy has made incontestable progress during the period of socialization, both as far as actual production is concerned and also in all that concerns the living standard of the peasants.

It is naturally hard to get accurate figures. M. Dumont has tried to squeeze out the truth as closely as possible. I have myself noticed that the revenue figures shown in the different kolkhozes visited were markedly higher than the mean figures given for the whole of the country in general studies of an official character. It may therefore be logically deduced; firstly that foreigners are only allowed to visit the most prosperous co-operatives, which is quite normal, and secondly that the official statistics must be fairly close to the truth. If the Chinese wanted to fake their statistics for the benefit of foreigners it would be relatively easy for them to fix their mean figures in accordance with the co-operatives accessible to visitors.

According to the official statements the general situation is as follows:

> 25 to 30 per cent of the rural population have reached a satisfactory standard of food and clothing.
> 15 per cent are still in need, from both points of view.

The majority, lying between these two extremes, have

enough food and clothing (although the standard cannot be considered satisfactory) and its condition is improving.[1]

The average annual agricultural income is estimated at 66 yuan per person (£9.18.0), an increase of 24 on the average income of 1954 (42 yuan). This calculation has been made on the basis of total agricultural production: 58,600 millions of yuan in 1956 (as against 32,500 millions in 1949) divided by the figure for the rural population (528 million in 1956 as against 470 million in 1949). It is therefore approximate.[2] This average figure is less than that resulting from calculations based on the different kolkhozes visited. For example the 'Red Light' kolkhoz near Sian which, in appearance, seemed to be poorest, shows 1,100,000 yuan income for 6,000 persons which, even allowing for a reserve fund of 100,000 yuan, represents a figure of more than 160 yuan per person. On the other hand this seems contradictory, but only from the point of view of the progress shown compared with the data published in the *Ta Kung Pao* of March 27th, 1957, which gives the average consumption as 72 yuan in 1952 increasing to 81 yuan in 1958; without doubt this is a question of consumption and not of income, but it is difficult to think that, in a society so poverty stricken and egalitarian, these two figures are not approximately the same.

But even if there has been progress (which, I repeat, seems

[1] An example of this classification, interesting rather in the evolution shown than in the distribution, is given in the study by Mr. Tan Cheng-Lin. However, this example seems considerably more favourable than the average. It deals with the Nunfeng co-operative in the district of Shuangshih in the province of Heilungkiang. Out of 343 persons, 45 are classed as 'poor', 122 as 'low standard' and 176 as 'higher standard' (thus in this case 50 per cent instead of 25 or 30 per cent). The evolution of the income of these three groups between 1954 and 1956 is given as follows:

	1954			1956		
	Income	*Expenses*	*Surplus*	*Income*	*Expenses*	*Surplus*
Poor	34·80	40·60	−5·80	77·07	64·10	+12·97
Low standard	52·80	51·80	+1·00	91·90	82·00	+9·90
High standard	69·30	62·80	+6·50	108·80	103·80	+5·80

[2] Article by Mr. Tan Cheng-Lin, Secretary of the Central Committee of the Chinese Communist Party, 'On the living standard of the Chinese peasant' reproduced in *Druzhba* of May 25th.

to me incontestable even if the figures themselves must be treated with reserve) in total production and living standards, it is no less certain that the rate of progress is decreasing from both these points of view. This has been confirmed to me personally by the Minister of Agriculture.

In these conditions, how can one envisage the future of Chinese agriculture without reverting to the problem of structure?

The margin of progress available with the present means of modernization (doubled harvests, crop rotation, thinning of plantings) which is already limited, will begin to diminish.

The application of other methods and particularly of mechanization, at present in its infancy, can only permit a small increase of production; its effect rather will be to limit the need for workers, to create agricultural unemployment and thus, at the best hypothesis, to provide a surplus of workers for transfer to the industrial sector.

Such an outlook cannot be considered satisfactory.

It is clear that China must obtain an increase of her agricultural production — and not merely the freeing of working forces for industry which is already amply provided.

Such an increase of production is necessary to raise the living standards of the agricultural population itself, since even according to the most official information 25 to 30 per cent only of the peasants have a sufficient standard, while 10 to 15 per cent are still poverty stricken.

But agricultural expansion is equally indispensable according to the universal law as a support for general economic expansion.

Without doubt the régime of collective economy permits, more easily than others, the blocking of consumption and of wages.[1]

But this rule cannot be absolute. Expansion will be greatly

[1] See chapter on: 'The Future of Communism in China and East-West Relations'.

facilitated by a certain margin of improvement in living standards. From another aspect, even more important, account must be taken of the exceptional demographic rhythm of China.

The supplementary workers must be fed, even if they are supernumary or useless, and even when they are unemployed. And the population temporarily unproductive, which is growing year by year, must also be fed.

Even to-day China is not safe from the catastrophes to which she has been accustomed for centuries; drought alternating with floods. This very year she has only just been able to avoid the 'spring famine'. Agricultural expansion being limited and not increasing, whereas demographic expansion is increasing and not limited, this risk, far from being eliminated, could be aggravated in the near future.

From this situation there is only one issue; the reclamation of new lands.

Can China undertake a large-scale enterprise similar to the Soviet enterprise of the '*tselina*', the reclamation of the virgin lands? One cannot see how she could find the vast mechanical means for an effort of this scale. That, in fact, was what the Minister of Agriculture replied to one of my questions. But can she, without going so far as such an enterprise, increase here and there her area of cultivable land? M. Dumont, who has written a thorough study of Chinese agriculture, estimates that this area could be doubled. I can only accept his view, doubtless more authoritative than that of the Chinese specialists themselves. Furthermore, the Chinese leaders must have the consciousness of this necessity and the will to make this effort.

Even in such a case, the agricultural economy seems to have two weak points:

1. One of these is stock-breeding. We have noted that since stock-breeding is little developed in China, her agri-

cultural economy has reacted less sharply than elsewhere to the 'insufficiencies' which mark the system of collective exploitation in this field. This is a fact. But expansion will certainly necessitate the development of stock-breeding, which has been neglected hitherto. There will then appear, without doubt, those disadvantages of which the most recent Soviet examples have shown the importance. But one must be fair; it is the communist economy which, in China, has been mainly occupied in developing this sector, especially for cattle. The merit of this conception is due to a system which seems badly adapted to its execution. Already as far as pigs, the traditional Chinese stock-breeding, are concerned, it seems that the period 1954–6 has shown a deficit and not an improvement (from 100 million head to 80 million head).

2. In the kolkhoz system the quality of the management is a decisive factor. An important Soviet personality told me, word for word: 'A kolkhoz is worth what its President is worth.' I cannot, naturally, give a personal and reasoned opinion on the quality of managers of co-operatives in China. The fact that they are recruited from among the militant communists is not in itself a guarantee of incapacity, but it does not guarantee that the most qualified administrator has been chosen. In this question, as in others, one of the principal problems to be faced in the new China is that of the quality of the executive cadres.

II. Industry[1] — Planning

The industrial modernization of China runs no risk of being faced with the same 'blocking' as the agricultural expansion. There is nothing here comparable to the limitation of cultivable lands.

We know, on the other hand, that régimes of collective

[1] I shall not touch on the question of craft production here. It represents about ten milliard yuan.

economy always encourage the equipment of basic and heavy industries; the risk here is not timidity but excessive ambition and consequent disequilibrium of the general planning effort. The example of China confirms this universal view.

There is no need of statistics to note the very great effort which has been undertaken and the important results which have already been achieved. They are more striking in the recently industrialized regions than in those where an infrastructure already existed (Manchuria). Thus I noted in the ancient capital of Sian, a city of the past, the impression made by a modern textile combine equipped with machinery which was all of Chinese make.

China, which has completed the great bridge over the Yang Tse Kiang and which is to tame the 'Yellow Dragon', which builds its own car factories and petrol refineries, is experimenting in the fields of automation but has had the common sense to assure, firstly, a national manufacture of bicycles. . . .

China proceeds, after the Soviet fashion, by five-year plans. The first such plan covers the years 1953–7 inclusive. According to official statistics, which do not appear to be contested, this plan has been carried out effectively, since it has been 81 per cent realized in the first four years. The outstanding 19 per cent should normally be completed in 1957. Certain official forecasts expect it to be over-fulfilled to 107 per cent, with 104 per cent for agriculture. But that seems to me optimistic.[1]

Industrial production as a whole seems to have increased by more than 80 per cent since 1952 over a very great starting figure, with a recession in 1955 and an upward rise in 1956.[2] The annual mean increase is 17 per cent (5 per cent for agriculture).

[1] See Huan Wei (*Druzhba*, May 29th).

[2] Annual increase:

1953 over 1952	31·7%	Publication of the Society of Far East Studies.
1954 over 1953	16·7%	
1955 over 1954	7·8%	
1956 over 1955	25·0%	

The figure for investment credits is very high and follows a sharply ascending curve, reaching 2,100 milliards of francs for 1956.[1]

It is significant to compare this with what has been done for agriculture.

In the seven years that have followed the Agrarian Reform, that is to say 1950 to 1956 inclusive, the government has devoted:

To irrigation	3,070 millions
To disaster relief, etc.	1,310 millions
To various other credits: extension of sowings, improvement of equipment, improvement of agricultural technique, struggle against plant diseases	1,280 millions
In all:	5,660 millions

And Mr. Tan Cheng-Lin, who gives these figures,[2] adds quite naturally:

'This sum represents a little more than 35 per cent of the total agricultural taxes paid by the peasants (16,000 million).'

One can imagine what French peasants would think if the total of agricultural credits represented only a third of the taxes on agriculture. . . .

However that may be for China, we see that all the effort made by the State, which expresses its satisfaction, is raised on a portion of the revenue that it draws from the peasants and that it represents, for seven years, a figure lower than that of the equipment credits for industry for a single year — and that the lowest.

We can see in these few figures both the scale of the effort

[1]
1953 - - - - - -	6,500 m.
1954 - - - - - -	7,500 m.
1955 - - - - - -	8,600 m.
1956 - - - - - -	14,000 m. or, in francs, 2,100 milliards.

(Total investments of the first plan: 42,740 m.)

[2] Article previously quoted.

for progress and also the principal planning errors that China, despite the Soviet example, has not been fully able to avoid (doubtless without this example the errors would have been even more grave).

1. A too ambitious global programme of investments in relation to the capacities of the economy.
2. An excessive proportion of 'heavy' investments as compared on the one hand to agriculture and on the other to light consumer industries.
3. Finally, in their application, the same excessive tendency has betrayed itself by the admission of certain too burdensome projects or projects of secondary utility, or carried out at too great an expense.

Thus this very year China has come to the brink of economic crisis, or perhaps such a crisis has already begun. It is hard to observe and forecast economic crisis in a country of collective economy and authoritarian administration. Can it be considered, as some specialists have pointed out, that it has already reached inflation? That is not my impression. I think that the Chinese economy has avoided the danger of real inflation, but it is probable that she has only been able to do so by drawing on her currency reserves and her stocks of raw materials almost to exhaustion.

This brings us to an evaluation of living standards. We have already mentioned this in connection with the peasants, who make up, it is true, a very important part of the population, at least 500 million persons (Mr. Tan Cheng-Lin estimates it at 528 million).

As far as the wage earners are concerned, it might be thought that a fairly regular increase in wages (the most recent was a 12½ per cent increase in June 1956) has kept pace more or less with the regular increases in prices. A more thorough study of this point would be very difficult. On the one hand wages are extremely variable, notably according to regions and the nature of enterprises; in the factories which I visited the average wage had been fixed at about 70 yuan a month, but it is certain that this figure is higher than the general mean (see Appendix I). The average wage in crafts and commerce, still based on the establishments visited, is appreciably lower, round about 40 yuan; but this too is certainly on the high side. According to the indications given in the *Ta Kung Pao* of March 22nd, 1957, the average annual expenditure per person would amount, among the wage-earning population, to the following:

1952 - - - -	151.0
1955 - - - -	164.0
1956 - - - -	179.6 (see Appendix II)

The evolution of prices is equally difficult to determine, for the lack of transport in China creates discrepancies very much greater than those we find in modern states. These discrepancies appear not only between regions, but even for every article the farther one gets from the centres of production. All in all, I am sure that I am not mistaken in assuming that price increases have almost entirely overstepped wage increases.

Finally, both as regards prices and wages, I think I may say without giving offence to our Chinese friends that the official reports often show grave discrepancies, as we have already noted with regard to agriculture.

Furthermore, a marked increase in consumption must follow from the regular increase in the population. This increase could have been largely covered by an increase in production had the investment effort not been so disproportionate. In these conditions, it has only been possible to face up to it by using the reserves of the national economy.

At the brink — or in the beginning — of the crisis and at the very moment of embarking upon the second and third five-year plans which are to cover the period 1958–68, it has been found necessary to go into reverse or, more exactly, to change course. This is the object of three different measures:

1. The total level of investments is to be markedly reduced from 1957, to the figure necessary to complete this plan, that is to say to seven or eight million instead of fourteen million.
2. The proportion between heavy industry investment on the one hand and investment in agriculture and light industry on the other is to be modified. The proportion for agriculture, which was 7·6 per cent of the investment total (5·9 per cent if one does not count the forestry industry) is to be raised to 10 per cent.
3. Lastly 'Economy' has been promoted to be the watchword alongside 'Production'. One can now read everywhere the watchword 'Production-Economy'. '*Production increasing in an atmosphere of economies and restrictions*', says Mr. Chen Yuan.

This motto has various applications.

This has led first of all to a renunciation of everything luxurious in the various investment categories. There have been criticisms (often with some reason) of too much luxury in construction, but it is to be feared that there is now some danger of falling into the opposite error. However that may be, it is now estimated that about 25 per cent of the majority of investments can be cut, above all in the non-productive categories.

It will now no longer be possible to put up such buildings as those I had been able to admire in Chunking: the stadium with its decorative roof and grand-stand, and above all the People's Hall, a sort of Coliseum which dominates the city with its bulbous cupola and is flanked by two colonnaded wings which form a luxury hotel. To-day they would be constructed much more simply or not at all. When I said to my guides in Chunking that they had been lucky to have been able to beautify their city before the new watchword, they agreed with a smile.

Certain investments which could not come under the heading of luxury but only of comfort and well-being will be postponed; residential buildings which are not indispensable, town-planning projects, scientific institutes, shops and warehouses, and even certain projects for schools and workers' tenements. It has been decided to make use of the existing towns and to develop them, rather than to create completely new ones.

They have even gone so far as to renounce certain grandiose projects for ultra-modern industrial centres, or at least to postpone them, in favour of a larger number of small and medium enterprises which could more easily be equipped from local resources.

'*It is more profitable for us to construct* (*at the same expense*) *fifteen little steelworks with a capacity of* 160,000 *tons each rather than construct a single huge combine of* 1,500,000 *tons capacity with highly mechanized and automatic equipment.*

'*We must abandon our present practice which consists in destroying old buildings and disposing of old equipment as scrap when we want to increase the production of older factories.*' (*Jen Min Jih Pao* of April 4th, 1957.)

It even seems that the completion of the projects put in hand by the Soviet Union — the 156 plus 55 (these last announced by Mr. Mikoyan in April 1956) — are to be slowed down. Without doubt, China would have more urgent need of Soviet aid for other matters.

But the economy watchword has yet another and vast field of application beside that of investments. Individuals are being invited to practise this virtue themselves. China, like the capitalist countries, is discovering the anti-inflationist properties of saving. Everywhere huge posters, depicting scenes of family life, urge the Chinese to practise this traditional virtue by subscribing to State Bonds or by putting their spare cash into Savings Bank accounts.

It is in no way surprising that China should have made

serious errors in planning or that she should be on the brink of economic crisis. These phenomena will certainly appear again. Without doubt collective economy magnifies errors in management and lends itself with greater difficulty to the compensating play of natural monetary mechanics. But mistakes and insufficiencies of this kind are not, however, limited to the socialist countries. And as far as economic crises are concerned. . . .

It must, however, be stressed that it is errors of degree and not errors of tendency that are in question. Contrary to what has sometimes been too easily assumed, the preferential development of heavy industry is in itself necessary — as long as it does not go so far as to risk bringing in its train the collapse of the economy or a too dangerous disequilibrium. This point is even more important in China than in the Soviet Union. For technically the Soviet Union can turn to reclamation of her virgin lands. China, as we have seen, cannot do so. For that she would need mechanical equipment and large-scale economic means. The credits devoted to these means are thus in reality more necessary and more profitable to agriculture than a superfluous inflation of credits destined, in the present state of affairs, to planting and the modernization of technique, of which the margin of utility, in default of new lands, finds itself every day more restricted. *There must be a fresh leap forward of heavy industry in order to give agriculture its chance. It will then permit a fresh development of the industrial economy.*

Having said this, it would be a serious error to think that China can see her economy collapse or even allow its expansion to be compromised.

To evaluate complacently the errors of the past, the difficulties of the present and the hazards of the future, to reckon on the disappearance of the régime or to justify absurd embargoes; if certain people cherish such ideas, they are singularly lacking not only in nobility but also in far-sightedness.

I am not in a position to say whether it will be in fifty years as some people believe, or sooner or later or never, that China will match the potential of the United States, which does not itself remain constant. Mr. Khrushchev, for his part, has just made a bet of limited scope and term; a competition in butter and meat production open for three years. We shall, after all, see for ourselves who will win. China's bet is of greater complexity; but the Chinese know how to wait.

What one can affirm without risk of error is that China will continue her expansion, and that she will surmount, more or less easily, more or less quickly, all her obstacles, like Mao Tse-Tung and his companions did in their Long March.

Faced with great problems, the People's China has, in fact, great means at her disposal. In default of our western aid, she has at her disposal the aid of the Soviet Union and all the peoples of the Eastern bloc (and, moreover, of the lessons drawn from their experience) and this aid, in case of necessity, is capable of being increased (it is admitted that the investment effort of the Soviet Union in China is not more than 1 per cent of her own investment effort).

She has at her disposal an immense labour reserve, disciplined, hard-working, frugal and inured to hardship, which can accomplish incredible results with the weakest material means (we have had proof of this, to our detriment, in the Korean war). Muscular energy indefinitely multiplied can accomplish prodigies. The builders of the Pyramids are on the job in the century of automation.

If the régime should ever collapse it will not be as a result of economic shocks. And it is not very likely that there will be such a collapse (let us think of the many vain prognostications since the beginning of the Soviet era in Russia). It can only progress by evolution; and this evolution will be determined and facilitated by success, and not by hindrances which can only retard it. China will resolve more or less well and more or less quickly all the problems of her industrial development and even those — more difficult — of her agricultural expansion. Such enthusiasm will not be curbed. China will sooner or later become a modern economic power. And once this is admitted, I think that it is in our interest that she does so sooner rather than later.

As in any case our attitude will never have more than a very small influence either way on this inevitable result, what interest have we in seeing it accomplished not only without us but against us!

APPENDIXES

UNIT of Currency: the Yuan (dollar) or J.M.P. (Jen Min Pao — money of the people).

Official exchange rates of the Bank of China: one Pound Sterling — Yuan (Y) 6.83, that is to say about 143 francs to the Yuan. For my calculation I have used the convenient figure of 150. (Previous to the last monetary revision.)

APPENDIX I

Wages and Living Conditions of Wage Earners

(Workmen, employees, officials)

1. The number of wage earners has increased from 15 million in 1952 to 24 million in 1956.

2. The annual wages bill, because of the general increase of 12½ per cent in June 1956, has risen from 9 to 10·7 thousand million yuan. This figure amounts to 43 per cent of the total expenses provided for in the budget of 1957. In 1956 the expenses provided for in the budget rose to 30,542 million yuan and the total of wages amounted to 34 per cent of this figure.

Wages vary according to regions and type of enterprise; an individual wage of 250 yuan per year can be considered as a minimum wage in the south, whereas it represents an average wage in the north of China.

Non-skilled workers - - -	Y. 100 to 300 annually
Skilled workers - - -	250 to 600 annually
Engineers* - - - -	600 to 1,800 annually
Heads of enterprises - - -	500 to 1,200 annually

* Some engineers are even better paid in certain jobs, such as oil prospectors, metallurgists, laboratory workers. Large enterprises guarantee accommodation, usually collective, for their personnel against a small deduction of 5 per cent to 7 per cent of their wages.

Appendix II

According to figures given in the daily newspaper *Ta Kung Pao* of May 1st, 1957, here is the apportionment of expenses for a family of six persons whose head is a skilled worker and whose wife also works (based on prices in August 1956).

Chinese noodles	25 kg.	Y. 9.42
Rice	30 kg.	8.40
Flour of medium quality	10 kg.	2.00
Oil	3 kg.	2.40
Salt	2 kg.	0.60
Fresh vegetables		9.00
Meat (pork)	1·75 kg.	2.00
Charcoal	250 pieces	4.50
Firewood	40 kg.	1.60
Rent, lighting, etc. (for two rooms and kitchen)		3.00
Various expenses including entertainment and transport		3.00
Clothing		2.50
Medical expenses		1.20
'Supplementary expenses for a birth'		4.00
		Y. 53.62

N.B. Certain of the items of this budget are markedly insufficient: meat, clothing and medical supplies (even though medical advice and simple medical remedies are free).

These living standards are only valid for the mass of wage earners, that is to say 24 million out of the 630 million Chinese (official population figure for the beginning of 1957).

Here are some complementary price figures:

Fruit (bananas at Canton)	Y. 0.05 apiece
Ordinary tea	8.00 per kg.
Ordinary cigarettes	0.25 the packet
Matches	0.20 the box
Transport: 3rd class railway	0.144 the klm.
Motor bus transport	0.36 the klm.
Local buses	0.18 the klm.

CONCLUSION

The Future of Communism in China and East-West Relations

CONTRARY to Marxist doctrine, I do not think that communism, wherever it has taken root, should be considered as a permanent phenomenon. But on the other hand to consider it, as an illustrious statesman did recently, as a transient phenomenon seems to me the result of wishful thinking (presuming, naturally, that one is speaking of the essence of the régime and not of this or that political attitude of its present leaders).

Between the 'permanent' and the 'transient' there is room for very variable time factors — and also for evolution for, despite the rigour of the doctrine, no régime can remain unchanged for ever. None the less, as we have seen, the present evolution of Chinese economy is not leading towards less communism but on the contrary to its fulfilment.

In considering the future of communism in China, three factors must be kept in mind:

1. The particular strength that the régime derives from the historical conditions of its establishment and the incontestable national renascence, both internal and external.
2. The structure of Chinese economy, as we have analysed it above, is peculiarly adapted to the country and thereby creates conditions more favourable than those which accompanied the introduction of communism in Soviet Russia (not to speak, naturally, of the other communist countries):

   in agriculture, because of the insignificance of stock-breeding, the sector most refractory to collective

methods of exploitation, and also because of the limited area of cultivable lands available and the needs of irrigation;
in petty trading, because of the abundance of distribution centres and because of the provincial maintenance 'outside the sector' of numerous middlemen;
in industry and commerce by the maintenance of experienced cadres of the bourgeoisie.

3. Finally, China despite her daily progress remains a country with a very backward economy from the threefold viewpoint of production, of technique and of the producers themselves (a mass of illiterates).

The impressions that I have gained from my trip to China confirm the views that I adopted after my trip to the Soviet Union and especially to former Turkestan (the Soviet Asian Republics).

Contrary to Marxist theory, a régime of collective economy is particularly suitable for backward countries, notably former colonies or semi-colonies. It is less and less suitable as economy develops and is modernized and as living standards rise. It is, at least in its absolutist form, almost insupportable for advanced economies.

This tentative opinion is easily explicable by logical analysis.

That communism finds a particularly favourable field in backward countries is primarily a result, *a contrario*, of the fact that, in these same countries, free capitalism brings a maximum of risk and a minimum of benefit.

The poor and inexperienced worker of the underdeveloped countries can with difficulty defend himself against the risks of exploitation inherent in this régime, whereas in advanced countries he finds efficient protection in trade union and even political action. Every 'colonial' nuance intensifies this phenomenon.

Inversely, this same poor and inexperienced worker can

benefit only in exceptional circumstances from the chances of promotion which amongst us are wide open, and can draw only a minor advantage or none at all from the individual political liberties which usually accompany free economy.

The essential problem to be resolved in the underdeveloped countries is the problem of investment. The most necessary investments are so considerable that they demand the blocking of consumption and, in consequence, of wages.

To ask the workers to increase their productivity and not to receive for themselves any of the benefits which result from this increase due to their own efforts, is incontestably easier in a system which eliminates profits, which equalizes sacrifices and which offers them, in default of anything better, the moral benefits of co-ownership (without counting, of course, the extreme possibilities of coercion).

The absence of infrastructure demands not only an enormous investment effort but also an order of priorities, a hierarchy, a discipline and, consequently, the limitation of private initiative in this field. This result is automatically attained by the system of collective economy (though often at the price of serious errors in planning). It can also, no doubt, be attained by certain procedures of guidance and intervention compatible with free economy, but with greater difficulty, when the economic structures have not acquired sufficient force.

A modern political democracy has more means of action on a vigorous capitalism than a mediaeval state on an anarchic capitalism.

It would be going too far to conclude from these observations that all backward countries are inevitably destined to communism. None the less, I think that if one wishes to turn them from this path, it is necessary to procure for them not only credits and experts, as has already been done, but also methods of exploitation which bring them advantages similar to those which they would find at once in a collective organization of their economy; for example the development of agricultural co-operatives of the French or even the Israeli type, and the socialization of basic sectors and the development of real formulas of mixed economy. It is equally necessary to avoid the reality, or even the appearance, of foreign economic colonization.

But even if it is possible to avoid the introduction of communism in those backward countries, where it has not already appeared, it is certainly much more difficult to eradicate it where it has already taken root. I will even go so far as to think that this is impossible by any outside obstructive action.

This result can only be attained — on the supposition that it is desired — by evolution. It is therefore necessary not to hinder but rather to encourage it.

In fact, when the infrastructure is organized, when the general situation is improved, then a raising of living standards becomes possible. A pressure more or less strong begins to exert itself despite ideological seductions or police restraints.

The standards of the producer rise with the same rhythm as those of production. A sense of demand follows the ascending curve of the norms.

Doubtless the communist state can still try to face up to these fresh exigencies. That is the explanation of the dramatic situation which to-day faces the Soviet Union. The principal accusation levelled against the 'anti-party' group was precisely its opposition to the personal interest in production of the members of the kolkhoz. Will the Khrushchev experiment succeed? It is too early to give an answer. But even if the communist régime succeeds in raising living standards, it will create, as progress advances, more and more marked 'insufficiencies' and 'bureaucratism', as it is fashionable to say to-day.

The collective system remains satisfying in its basic sectors and large-scale enterprises; the reclamation of thousands of hectares of virgin lands, electrical or mining equipment, large-scale industry.

But the motive force of personal interest and, above all, the genius of private initiative are, in my opinion, irreplaceable in certain agricultural sectors, in commerce, in the consumer industries and in quality production. The compass of socialist economy can only with difficulty result in the final satisfaction of personal and differentiated needs.

The producer has his demands as a producer, but he has also demands as a consumer and is ready to make further demands as a citizen, for the parallel raising and consolidation of his standard of life leads him the more eagerly to make demands of a spiritual nature.

By the very logic of its achievements, collective economy creates the factors valid for a free or mixed economy. Communism which has sometimes transformed, sometimes eliminated, capitalists is also capable of manufacturing them.

History, moreover, teaches us that primitive societies easily welcome communal methods. Mr. Khrushchev said recently, with his taste for vivid phrases and his customary assurance, that socialism would succeed capitalism as capitalism had feudalism with the inevitability . . . of a gynaecological process. It might, however, be thought that in any case the term of gestation was strangely indeterminate. But could not the reverse process be imagined? A communist society having obtained, as such, a certain improvement of living standards might beget liberal and semi-capitalist methods of exploitation?

Even if one does not go so far as accepting this conclusion as definite, how can one deny, after the Soviet example (not to speak of the communist countries of Central Europe) the existence of a tendency towards a non-communist system, or at least towards a communist system of a new type?

So I repeat that instead of hindering this evolution we should aid it.

In it lies the only chance not only of a final reconciliation of the different economic systems (for my part I believe that this reconciliation will take place at a common level) but also of a better understanding between the peoples and an international political détente.

We must radically reconsider our policy towards East-West relations and more particularly, since that is my theme, towards the People's China. It is surely paradoxical that our attitude towards this country should be infinitely more severe than towards the Soviet Union which has recently given us subjects of conflict which are much sharper and which faces us daily with the most formidable problems.

The key problem of Formosa must be settled as soon as possible.

Without doubt this problem mainly concerns the People's China, the United States and the local authorities on Formosa. But it necessarily interests the other western countries whether they have, like Great Britain, recognized China (even though this recognition has not yet resulted in normal relations), or whether they have not yet recognized her, like France. It is of essential interest to what might be called western strategy which has here met with the most serious of checks; division in inertia.

From my interviews with the Chinese leaders I have the very clear impression that the status of Formosa is capable of a reasonable solution. This solution is possible to-day. As time works for them, they can only prove more difficult to treat with to-morrow. They do not dream of conquering the island by force of arms, and who could dream of reconquering the continent? And the recent Taipeh incidents have helped to open many eyes.

Must one foresee international control, temporary status, elections? It would be rash for a simple observer to make prognostications on so delicate a negotiation; what matters is to begin it. There can be no question of imposing on populations a destiny that they reject, nor even of sacrificing men, even though they represent a fault perpetuated rather than a sovereignty abolished.

There are also sources of bitterness that remain, and painful human questions to resolve. But it would be a mistake to engage in negotiations between the West and China while limiting them to particular problems or specific objectives.

Our principal trump, at the moment, is to renounce a fiction. Not merely the fiction of the China of Taipeh as the fifth power in the world and a permanent member of the Security Council, for it is difficult to believe in it any longer, even were it in the Platonic cavern of the shades; but the substantive fiction of 'the two Chinas'. It is that which so preoccupies them and they do not hide the fact. In our hands this fiction still has an exchange value. Soon it will have less; soon it will have none at all.

One serious objection is, I am told, the fear lest such a settlement might increase to an exaggerated degree — and to the detriment of the western powers — the prestige of the People's China among the Chinese colonies in other Asian lands and even among the governments and peoples of those countries. Is it not, on the contrary, by taking the initiative that we might surely forestall any disequilibrium of this type? Such a transaction carried out in a spirit of realism, far-sightedness and even generosity would surely bring more credit to the West than an obstinate policy of awaiting the inevitable.

With or without an increase of prestige, it is clear that China will not for a long time have at her disposal an economic potential greater than her own needs, which are immense. For long she could not make available from her own resources aid intended for the other Asian countries. The West and, obviously, the United States above all would have at its disposal, without competition, the trump of external aid. And can one believe for a single moment that this aid would be morally or politically less beneficial because it would be granted to these backward countries *for* themselves in a spirit of generosity and human solidarity, rather than *against* anyone, in a negative and to some extent defensive prejudice?

Our success will be the more assured if we can extend this

aid, this feeling of solidarity, to that one of the underdeveloped countries of Asia which makes the greatest contribution from her own energies and her own resources, namely — China.

With or without a settlement on Formosa (but everything would be very different should this settlement be made) it is necessary to free and to develop relations of every kind, economic and cultural, with China. I regret that on this point I am in contradiction with a statesman for whom I have the greatest respect.[1] Our attitude of resistance and refusal produces a result quite contrary to what we wish to obtain.

China must be aided in the immense effort which her people are making to get out of the rut of backwardness that has existed for several centuries. She must be helped to accomplish her modernization, for only that modernization can bring her closer to us, economically and politically.

She must be helped, because the awareness of the Chinese leaders and the Chinese people of our measures to aid them will be in itself a very great advance along this path.

The underdeveloped peoples and the peoples who have only recently acquired their independence are easily offended. For China, the extraordinary contrast between her overwhelming resources and her profound archaism in the light of her new will to live, creates a complex of pride and modesty, a mixture of despondency and of confidence, that I have observed in Mao Tse-Tung and, consequently, this oversensitiveness may be carried to extremes.

We have renounced, happily moreover, military strategy. Are we to renounce psychological strategy also?

Perhaps my stay in China has given me a taste for allegory; I would like to end by evoking a river, the Yang Tse Kiang, and two animal figures, the Serpent and the Tortoise.

The Serpent and the Tortoise are two promontories, so called after their form, which face one another on the two

[1] Cf. statement by Mr. Foster Dulles of June 29th.

opposite banks of the Yang Tse Kiang at the precise point where there has just been constructed, between the twin cities of Wuchang and Hankow, a gigantic bridge.

This bridge is one of the great achievements of the régime. It is 1,155 metres long with piers fitted with lifts and with a roadway and a railway on two superimposed platforms. It has been built from whatever materials were to hand and is, according to the technicians, a most remarkable work.

It is a work of great economic importance for it creates the only transverse highway of China. But it is also an ideal and a symbol.

Twenty years ago, in 1937, during the hours of the Long March, while he composed on horseback little poems according to the mannered rules of prosody of the twelfth century, Mao Tse-Tung evoked the river and its curious promontories. This winding ribbon, he said, cut China into two nations foreign to one another. The Serpent and the Tortoise watch one another and watch endlessly....

Then, in 1956, Mao Tse-Tung composed on the same theme a new poem. The Serpent and the Tortoise still watch endlessly, but men will throw from one to the other a bridge of iron....

This thought is to-day, as Valéry would say, 'remarkably achieved'.

Are capitalism and communism going to face each other indefinitely and watch one another like these two promontory figures from the opposite sides of a liquid frontier? Or are we to admit that they correspond to different stages of the technical life of humanity and that it is possible to establish a link between the one and the other?

Between East and West, as between the Serpent and the Tortoise, are we to throw a bridge? So that one day 'men will forget that once was here an impassable chasm'.

PRINTED IN GREAT BRITAIN
BY ROBERT MACLEHOSE AND CO, LTD
THE UNIVERSITY PRESS, GLASGOW